UNDERSTANDING
THE
Holy Spirit
TODAY

Also by Doris Wynbeek Rikkers

Bibles

*The Wayfinding Bible: Helping You
Navigate God's Word*

*The Family Reading Bible: Lead Your
Family through God's Word*

Children's Books

The Spirit of God Illustrated Bible

Read with Me Bible for Toddlers

Little Jesus, Little Me

*Read with Me Bible: An NIrV Story Bible
for Children*

Read with Me Bible for Little Ones

God Loves Me Baby Bible (as Susan
Elizabeth Beck)

God Loves Me Bible (as Susan Elizabeth Beck)

UNDERSTANDING THE *Holy Spirit* TODAY

A BIBLICAL PERSPECTIVE OF GOD'S POWER AND ACTION

DORIS WYNBEEK RIKKERS

New York   Nashville

FaithWords
Hachette Book Group
1290 Avenue of the Americas, New York, NY 10104
faithwords.com
twitter.com/faithwords

First Edition: September 2018

FaithWords is a division of Hachette Book Group, Inc. The FaithWords
name and logo are trademarks of Hachette Book Group, Inc.

The publisher is not responsible for websites (or their content)
that are not owned by the publisher.

Library of Congress Cataloging-in-Publication Data

Names: Rikkers, Doris, author.
Title: Understanding the Holy Spirit today : a biblical perspective of
    God's power and action / Doris Wynbeek Rikkers.
Description: first [edition]. | New York : Faith Words, 2018.
Identifiers: LCCN 2018011726| ISBN 9781455571819 (trade pbk.) |
    ISBN 9781455571802 (ebook)
Subjects: LCSH: Holy Spirit—Biblical teaching.
Classification: LCC BS680.H56 R55 2018 | DDC 231/.3—dc23
LC record available at https://lccn.loc.gov/2018011726

ISBN: 978-1-4555-7181-9 (trade paperback), 978-1-4555-7180-2 (ebook)

Printed in the United States of America

LSC-C

10 9 8 7 6 5 4 3 2 1

The Spirit Today

Where can I go from your Spirit?
Where can I flee from your presence?
If I go up to the heavens, you are there;
if I make my bed in the depths, you are there.
If I rise on the wings of the dawn,
if I settle on the far side of the sea,
even there your hand will guide me,
your right hand will hold me fast.

Psalms 139:7–10

Contents

Introduction

Many Christians believe in God and have a personal relationship with Jesus Christ, God's Son. They understand those two persons of the Trinity—God is the Creator and Father, Jesus is the Son who came to earth as a human, suffered, and died for us. But then there's the other person of the group—the Holy Spirit, he came in later, right?—at Pentecost, to start the church. Yes, that's true, but there's more than that. The Spirit's work is far greater than most Christians realize.

Understanding the Holy Spirit Today is a book that will help you grow in your knowledge of the Spirit's work in the Bible. Just as we teach our young children about Jesus by first sharing with them the stories of Jesus and what he did, so too we must begin our understanding of the Spirit by reading the stories of what he accomplished and how he acted throughout

God's story and the history of his people. With a foundation of basic knowledge, we can then move on to a greater understanding of the Spirit and discern his presence in our everyday lives.

The Bible tells us that God's Spirit is everywhere—he rides on the wings of the dawn, he settles on the far side of the sea, he lives in the heavens high above the earth, and he fills the deepest hollows on the ocean floor. There is no place in the universe where we can escape from the safety and comfort of his presence. Since the Spirit is alive and active all around us, we should be familiar with his actions, his gifts, and his abilities. Unfortunately, too often we shy away from knowing the Spirit, perhaps because we fear "getting carried away" by him. And yet if we desire a close relationship with God, we must learn more about all three persons of the Trinity: God the Father, God the Son, and God the Holy Spirit.

God's Spirit is the "worker bee" of the Trinity—he does the work of God's mind and plan. He was right next to God at the dawn of creation. He provided the breath that made Adam come to life. He filled people with extraordinary strength and skills to do wondrous things for God. He equipped leaders with talents to guide God's people. He supplied ordinary people with the words of the Lord to instruct, correct, and give hope for the future. Depending on context, the Hebrew word *ruach* can be translated as Spirit, breath, or wind. But without the work of the Spirit, breath is only a physical reflex that moves air in and out of the lungs, and wind is only air in motion. The Spirit transforms everything, filling breath, wind, and the human spirit with something powerful and divine.

Sometimes the Spirit is quiet and gentle, hovering in the background. Sometimes he is loud and powerful, making his presence obvious. At first he fueled people with just enough strength to accomplish a momentary task. Then God promised to send his Spirit through the prophets to give his people a new heart. Finally the Spirit Counselor came to create a new community—the church—and to stay in people's hearts forever.

When God calls one of us to do something great for him, we don't have to fret about achieving it on our own. God will send his Great Powerful Spirit to be with us and give us the strength, the confidence, the power to accomplish his plan. Just as the Spirit aided people in the Bible to do extraordinary things for God, so too he will do it for us today.

One thing is for sure: God's Spirit is living among us. He always was, always is, always will be. This book is designed to help you recognize and understand the work of the Holy Spirit, and lift your awareness of this person of the Trinity who is often overlooked. By reading his stories in the Bible and realizing how he works in our lives today, may you come to know him better.

PART ONE

The Spirit's Work in the Old Testament

The Spirit first manifested his work on the day of creation. Up until the time God uttered the first words to bring forth the light from the darkness, the Spirit was hovering, waiting for God to speak. It was then that the Spirit brought about what God directed and desired for the universe and the elements of nature. The Spirit's work continued throughout the Old Testament stories, first in his interaction with creation, then in his infusion of life into humans, and finally in the lives of the people God selected to be his own special nation. While the Spirit's actions are continuous through nature, his presence was intermittent with God's chosen people. As God selected Abraham, the Spirit's focus shifted beyond creation in general to people, specifically God's people—those whom the Spirit would establish and preserve through generations to bring about God's plans and purposes. The Spirit provided skills and talents, sometimes enhancing what was already there and making it better. He transformed timid individuals into courageous ones, weak into strong, ordinary into extraordinary. He gave prophets the right words to speak because they spoke for God. His presence and power were selective—provided to only a few, remaining sometimes for a moment, sometimes for a span of time, occasionally for a lifetime. The Spirit came and worked in a person, then he departed. He moved people to action or actively and physically transported them from place to place. During the time of the exile, when God's people were scattered, the Spirit spoke through the prophets and promised a brighter future: one day the Spirit, a new Spirit, would come to live in people's hearts and stay with them forever.

Chapter One

The Work of the Spirit in Creation and Nature

"The whole of creation is a fabric woven by the Spirit, and is therefore a reality to which the Spirit gives form."

Jürgen Moltmann

The Spirit stood with God at the dawn of creation. God created; the Spirit designed, ordered, and perfected what God called into being. Then the Spirit sustained all that had been created; nothing reverted to the chaos of the past. As soon as God created Adam from the dust of the ground, the Spirit breathed the breath of life into him, signifying that humans were indeed in God's image and belonged to him alone.

When God's disappointment in humans reached a pinnacle of despair, he chose to destroy everything with a flood. The Spirit stepped in and started his work. First he helped Noah believe God's command to build an ark before the first drop of rain. Then he withdrew the order imposed on the waters of the earth, causing the chaos of the watery abyss to return. He withdrew the breath of life from all animals and humans, except for Noah and his family; to them he brought comfort as they faced the confines of the ark and an uncertain future. After the rain ceased, the Spirit restored the design originally intended: oceans and rivers flowed again within their shores and banks, and the waters receded. The wind that blew across the earth contained his power, which dried out the land. And finally the Spirit renewed the face of the earth.

The Spirit Brings Order and Breathes Life

from Genesis 1–2

While God's Spirit hovered close by, waiting to hear the words that would bring everything into being, God stood on the edge of endless darkness and announced, "Let's create a world." Then God called out across the darkness, "Let light shine." And glorious light pierced the darkness.

God separated the water so the sky was above and the water below. The Spirit moved over the deep, dark water as a hummingbird hovers over a blossom in summer. Then God said to the water on earth, "Gather together in the places I show you so that dry

> Now the earth was formless and empty, darkness was over the surface of the deep, and the Spirit of God was hovering over the waters. (Genesis 1:2)

ground appears." And the water obeyed and gathered itself into streams and rivers, lakes large and small, and the great seas and oceans of the world. And the dry places became the great lands of the continents, with steep mountains, deep valleys, flat sandy deserts, wide prairies, and rolling hills. At God's command plants grew and trees covered the mountains, flowers and grasses carpeted the prairies, fruit trees and grapevines filled the valleys, palm trees and cacti grew in the dry deserts. Then God looked around at all he had created and said, "This is good."

Then God created the sun to mark the day and the moon to light the night. He flung millions of stars across the darkness to light up the heavens and decorate the sky. And his Spirit brought order and design to the universe, arranging the stars in orderly patterns to form the constellations. He secured the planets in their rotations and orbits. He patterned the seasons and the predictable tides and currents of the oceans.

Then God viewed the sky and said, "Let creatures large and small fly in the sky and overflow the waters." Birds filled the air with melodious songs and colorful wings. Fish jumped in ponds, swam in lakes, and navigated the streams. Whales glided along the ocean's currents, and starfish and crustaceans crept on the floors of the seas.

God's voice spread across the land: "Let creatures with the breath of life in them sprawl out." And the creatures and animals of the world took their places on the earth. They filled the forests, wandered the plains, and perched on mountain peaks. God looked at all that he had created and said, "This is really good."

Through God's words the world began. And by God's Spirit each moment and object of creation stayed in its appointed position. The Spirit's work as sustainer of the universe kept the light constant, not allowing it to morph back into its former darkness. The land stayed dry, and water remained in the oceans and lakes. In the morning the sunshine brought a new day, and at night the moon and stars lit up the sky. Winter melted into spring, spring blossomed into summer, summer eased into fall, and fall merged with winter. Seeds scattered on the wind, established themselves, and produced new plants. All things and all crea-tures continued as they had been created. Noth-ing disappeared, because God's Spirit kept every-thing the way God had created it.

> Then the LORD God formed a man from the dust of the ground and breathed into his nostrils the breath of life, and the man became a living being.
> (Genesis 2:7)

God's great world was ready to receive the ulti-mate in God's creativity.

> The Spirit of God has made me; the breath of the Almighty gives me life. (Job 33:4)

And God announced, "Let's make people who are in our likeness so they can take care of this glorious world." Then he scooped up dust from the ground and formed a man. And the Spirit breathed the breath of life into the man, and he came alive. Then God made a companion for the man from one of his ribs. And God's Spirit breathed life into the woman, and she came alive. The man's name was Adam and the woman's name was Eve. The breath of life from God's Spirit filled them and caused them to inhale and exhale continuously, day by day, night after night. They did this automatically, without any effort, with no thought. The Spirit's breath of life continued in them and allowed them to live.

God planted a beautiful garden named the Garden of Eden and placed Adam and Eve in the lush greenery of the garden along with the animals and a variety of plants and fruits to eat. God walked with Adam and Eve in the garden each evening. And his Spirit lived within them. The Spirit's presence filled the garden with peace, allowing Adam and Eve to live comfortably and freely in their custom-made paradise.

The Spirit Today

The Spirit is continuously at work in nature today. We might not think about it at all, but every time we plant our feet on the floor first thing in the morning, gravity works, and our feet stay planted right where we've placed them. Humans have relegated this phenomenon to their knowledge of science, crediting "Mother Nature" or the natural order. We expect the day to be a twenty-four-hour span, the night to display the moon and the stars in expected patterns. We take the seasons for granted and assume nature will continue as usual. The natural order continues because the Spirit sustains the works of creation.

As sure as we are of the patterns of nature— seasons, tides, planets in stationary orbits—so too we are certain of breathing. Rarely do we think about inhaling and exhaling. Our first breath is momentous, and so is our last, but in between we breathe with no conscious effort or awareness. Certainly asthma attacks, bronchitis, or severe colds increase our awareness of our breathing, but under most circumstances, breathing is not our focus; we take it for granted. But all breath comes from the Spirit. He is the originator of our breath and our being and thus makes all humans in God's image. Take a moment; breathe deeply. We all need to be more mindful of these expected norms as the Spirit's presence in the world around us.

The Spirit Withdraws and Renews

from Genesis 6:5–9:17

Over many years the humans God had created multiplied and populated the earth, just as he had commanded them to do. But evil entered the world when Adam and Eve disobeyed God in the Garden of Eden, and eventually most humans completely forgot about God.

Then the LORD said, "My Spirit will not contend with humans forever, for they are mortal; their days will be a hundred and twenty years." The LORD regretted that he had made human beings on the earth, and his heart was deeply troubled." (Genesis 6:3, 6)

After a long time, the world was full of evil, and God no longer thought of his creation as good. In fact, he regretted that he had even made humans in the first place. So he made a decision: he would destroy all the humans, all the animals, everything that contained the breath of life, by inundating the world with water.

By faith Noah, when warned about things not yet seen, in holy fear built an ark to save his family. (Hebrews 11:7)

However, one person, an upright and good man named Noah, still revered God, so God warned him about the coming flood, instructing him to build a colossal boat to save himself, his family, and a collection of animals. Believing what God told him, Noah started constructing a boat according to God's blueprint even as Noah's neighbors ridiculed him for his foolish endeavor. The construction being complete,

Noah gathered two of every species of animal from all over the land and settled them inside the boat along with his family.

When everyone was safe inside, God himself sealed the entrance to the boat to secure those inside from the water. Then God's Spirit, who had sustained the powers of nature, withdrew his control over the earth, and chaos erupted. The heavens broke open and torrents of rain poured out of the sky. The earth split apart and water gushed from subterranean sources. Oceans surged and water spilled over the banks of the rivers. The waters of the deep merged with the waters on the earth's surface, covering every inch of dry land. As if God had never said, "Let dry ground appear," the world became its original watery, chaotic self. Torrential rain continued for forty days and forty nights.

The Spirit withdrew his life-giving breath from the world, and all the living creatures died. Only eight people still breathed the breath of life: Noah, his wife, and his three sons and three daughters-in-law. They were safe inside the boat, sustained by God's Spirit.

> If God were to take back his spirit and withdraw his breath, all life would cease, and humanity would turn again to dust. (Job 34:14–15 NLT)

Noah, his family, and all the animals were safe from the watery mess that swirled across the land, filling the deepest valleys and covering the highest mountains. For five long months Noah's boat rode the waves of the ocean and drifted across the water that covered the earth. The Great Comforter, the Spirit, remained with the boat and its passengers. His presence was both powerful and calming, saving the animals and the people from the devastation of the floodwaters.

Then God remembered Noah and all the animals alive in the boat. The destruction of the world and its inhabitants was over. It was now time to revive those who remained alive. God's Spirit, the same one that had hovered over the waters at creation, resumed his control over the world, becoming a mighty wind that blew across the earth. The Spirit-Wind directed the water of the rivers and streams, lakes and ponds, oceans and seas to return to their original places. The waters below the ground quieted down and returned to their sources. Once again, as in the beginning, dry ground appeared.

Eventually Noah's boat drifted toward the mountains of Ararat and perched on a ridge. Another month passed as Noah sent out birds to determine the condition of the land. When the ground was finally dry, God told Noah to leave the safety of the boat. Then Noah opened the door and released the animals into the new world.

The Spirit was at work, making the world new again. He turned the gray and muddy muck into color-filled landscapes. He put the orderly patterns of life back into place. Once again grasses filled the meadows, flowers bloomed, and trees grew.

> When you send your Spirit, [all creatures] are created, and you renew the face of the ground. (Psalm 104:30)

Then God made Noah a promise: "As long as the earth endures, seedtime and harvest, cold and heat, summer and winter, day and night will never cease." God sealed his promise with a sign—a multicolored rainbow that arced across the sky.

The Spirit Today

Frightening, isn't it, to think about a world-encompassing flood? We all know about floods, the havoc they wreak on people's lives and the devastation they cause. Floods continue year in and year out, due to vicious storms or seasonal thaws after harsh winters.

But the flood of the Bible was unlike any flood ever known to humans. Not only did it encompass the entire world, it was caused because God's Spirit *stopped* doing what he was expected to do; he withdrew his sustaining power so that the world returned to its chaotic precreation condition. But don't worry, a repeat performance will not occur—God has promised never to send a world-destroying flood again. He even sealed the promise with the sign of the rainbow. God's Spirit will continue his work in nature, preventing an extreme, world-encompassing catastrophe and utter chaos. The next time you see a rainbow, remember God's promise and the sustaining work of this Spirit in creation.

The Spirit-Wind Divides the Sea

from Exodus 13–14

> Where is he who set his Holy Spirit among them, who sent his glorious arm of power to be at Moses' right hand, who divided the waters before them, to gain for himself everlasting renown, who led them through the depths? (Isaiah 63:11–13)

God instructed his people to migrate to Egypt in order to save them from a worldwide famine. During the four hundred years God's people lived in Egypt, God blessed them with strong and healthy offspring, establishing them as a great nation. Fearing their numbers and potential power, Pharaoh subjected God's people to hard labor, manufacturing bricks and constructing the great cities of Egypt. The Hebrew people worked hard every day, and they were miserable because of their intense forced labor. In desperation they prayed to God, asking him to deliver them.

God selected a man named Moses to represent him before Pharaoh, and to convince the ruler that God's people needed to leave Egypt to worship their God in the desert. As it turned out, Pharaoh needed a lot of convincing. Ten times God displayed his greatness and power through miracles called plagues to Pharaoh and all the people in Egypt, but Pharaoh stubbornly refused to yield to God's power and request. Finally, after the tenth plague, when people actually died, Pharaoh agreed to let the people go.

As soon as Pharaoh granted them permission to leave, God's people exited Egypt in a hurry and headed into the desert. Soon they encountered an expanse of water that blocked their escape route. The

Red Sea was in front of them, and Pharaoh's army was on the move, closing in behind them.

"We're going to die!" the people shouted at Moses. "Why did you bring us here? Now what will we do?"

"Stay calm, stand still, and see what God will do," Moses said to the restless crowd. "We are not alone. Look again at God's cloud hovering over us and the fire that assures us of his presence. God's Spirit is here with us. Watch what happens."

That night a strong and powerful wind blew across the desert from the east. The Great Spirit-Wind that had hovered over the waters at creation came again. The Spirit-Wind that had dried out the land after the Great Flood now blew across the waves of the sea. The Saving Spirit who had saved Noah, who had renewed the land and brought life back to the earth, was there to save God's people.

All night long the wind blew. It banked the water to the right and the left, dividing the sea and making a path through the water. The water stood up as firm as a concrete wall, and the sand below was dry and hard. "Look!" the people cried in amazement. "There's a dry path leading through the water!" And all the people with their wagons and carts, animals, and children crossed the great sea on dry ground.

No one got wet, no one sank into the sandy bottom of the sea. The Spirit-Wind held the sea back and kept the path firmly packed down and dry.

When everyone was safely on the opposite shore, the people turned around and looked back. "Oh no," they screamed. "Look! Pharaoh's army is coming the same way we did!"

Pharaoh had changed his mind and wanted his slaves back in Egypt. His army, with its horses and chariots, had stormed across the desert and onto the path through the sea. The entire army was far from shore when suddenly something changed. The Spirit-charged wind stopped blowing. The sand that had stayed firm and dry while the Israelites marched across now got soft and wet. Dry turned back to soggy. Chariot wheels and horses' hooves sank deep in the sand as the army struggled to turn around. The firm walls of the sea began to break apart, and water crashed down over the Egyptian horses, the chariots, and the weapon-laden soldiers. The waves swallowed them up, and the Egyptian warriors disappeared.

God's Spirit had returned the sea to its normal place. Pharaoh's army was destroyed, and God's people were safe on the opposite shore of the Red Sea.

The Spirit Today

Our minds have difficulty with the thought of a mighty wind that not only divides a sea overnight and dries out the sand so a million people can race across but also holds back walls of water and then reverses it all in an instant. Spectacular displays of God's power usually don't happen on this scale in our lives, but it is at work there. God's Spirit might not move walls of water or dry out sand for us, but he does come. He comes to us in the quiet of the night to protect us, to clarify our situation, and to solve our problems. My mother used to say, "Sleep on it. It will be clearer in the morning." And she was usually right. Perhaps it was the rest that helped, but more likely it was the Spirit moving in the night, presenting a solution to the problem by morning. The next time you go to bed with a problem, leave it to God. Trust that the Spirit still moves in our lives to solve problems in the night, to bring clarity and inspiration as we, like the Israelites on the water's edge, remain still.

Chapter Two

The Work of the Spirit in God's People

"The Holy Spirit blows where he will, not following merits but producing them."

Herman Bavinck

The Spirit was active in God's plan for his people and their story. He moved Abraham out of his comfort zone and into the unknown to follow God and believe his promises to give Moses land and build him into a great nation. He provided confidence, faith, and special talents required for the building of family and nation to Abraham, Isaac, and Jacob in spite of life's difficulties and circumstances. As God's people grew into a great nation during their time in Egypt, the Spirit sustained the faith of the people and enabled them to live lives that didn't make sense to the people around them. He was with God's people as they left Egypt, showing his force and power in the wind that parted the Red Sea and creating a dry path. Then he gave special talents to Israel's leaders to govern the people and to craftsmen to build the Tabernacle so God could dwell among his people. His influence moved insignificant, ordinary people to have the confidence, ability, and power to do great things for God.

The Spirit Selects Abraham

from Genesis 12:1–9

After the Flood humans had once again populated the world. They had spread out across the land, grouping themselves into tribes and nations. They had built great cities and civilizations. One day God selected a man named Abraham and his wife Sarah from Mesopotamia to be the father and mother of his own special nation. God planned to shower them with blessings, but his requirements were steep. He asked them to wander rather than be settled in one place, to live in a tent rather than in a house built of solid stone, to live with uncertainty, to go where no one had gone before, and to live God's way, by God's guidance, rather than by the rules of humans.

> [Stephen said,] "The God of glory appeared to our father Abraham while he was still in Mesopotamia, before he lived in Harran. 'Leave your country and your people,' God said, 'and go to the land I will show you.'" (Acts 7:2–3)

Abraham could not have chosen to do this on his own; it went against all he had ever known. It was an illogical thing to do, incompatible with everything he cherished. It was God's Spirit who made Abraham say "Yes, I will go" when anyone else would have stayed in a civilized place. The Spirit made Abraham willing to step out in faith and head out into the desert, wandering to a place only God knew. Through Abraham's move a people would live differently, under God's direction to be God's great nation, and through them everyone else in the world would be blessed.

> By faith Abraham, when called to go to a place he would later receive as his inheritance, obeyed and went, even though he did not know where he was going. (Hebrews 11:8)

God's Spirit worked inside Abraham's heart and mind to help him believe that this was the right thing to do. So Abraham packed up his wife, gathered his servants and their families, herded the camels, the donkeys, and the sheep, and departed civilization. He headed into the desert to follow wherever God's Spirit led.

The Faith-Building Spirit worked silently, deep in the hearts and minds of Abraham, his son Isaac, and his grandson Jacob. The Faith Builder worked in their lives, sustaining them and keeping them strong in their belief in God, helping them follow him and his commands. They were imperfect people, but through his Spirit, God worked his plan, slowly and steadily building a great nation.

The Spirit Today

God selected Abraham from all the nations and peoples of the world and then provided him with the wisdom to obey the voice that called him to change everything about his life. Faith is the work of the Spirit. The Bible tells us that "faith is confidence in what we hope for and assurance about what we do not see" (Heb. 11:1) and that "by faith Abraham, when called to go to a place he would later receive as his inheritance, obeyed and went, even though he did not know where he was going" (Heb. 11:8). Through the work of the Spirit, faith came to the people in the Old Testament. Today the Spirit continues to instill faith in unbelievers as he once did for Abraham. His presence with us is our seal of approval, showing we belong to God. By sending his Spirit to us, God tells us that we are his children and nothing can separate us from his love. "[God] anointed us, set his seal of ownership on us, and put his Spirit in our hearts as a deposit, guaranteeing what is to come" (2 Cor. 1:21–22).

The Spirit Gives Joseph Special Gifts

from Genesis 37, 39–41

But it is the spirit in a person, the breath of the Almighty, that gives them understanding. (Job 32:8)

Abraham's grandson Jacob had many sons—twelve in all: Reuben, Simeon, Levi, Judah, Dan, Naphtali, Gad, Asher, Issachar, Zebulun, Joseph, and Benjamin.

The Spirit of God came upon one of Abraham's grandsons in a special way: Joseph had unusual dreams and, over time, the Spirit also gave him the ability to know their meaning. While Joseph was a young man, he couldn't discern the meaning of his dreams, but he still enjoyed sharing them with his brothers, who did not appreciate the implications of Joseph's nighttime visions. Nor did they appreciate that their father had chosen Joseph as his favorite son and provided Joseph with a special multicolored coat. Whenever Joseph wore the special coat, his brothers were reminded that Joseph, not any of them, was their father's favorite.

One morning, adorned in his coat, Joseph paraded in front of his brothers and said, "Listen to this. I had this dream last night. We were at work in the fields cutting and gathering grain and binding it into sheaves. Suddenly my sheaf of grain stood up as straight as a tree, and your sheaves went limp. They bent over, pointing in the direction of my sheaf, like they were bowing down."

Of course the older brothers hated the idea of their bowing down to their younger brother. In fact, the idea made them so angry, they hated Joseph even more than previously.

When Joseph had another dream, he eagerly told

his brothers and father about it. "I had another dream last night," he announced. "This time the sun, the moon, and eleven stars circled around me and bowed down!"

Of course the brothers hated that dream even more than the first one. They were furious and shouted at Joseph, "How dare you think that we, your older brothers, will bow down to you! Do you really think you'll be someone important someday and make us beg in front of you?"

Sometime later, as the brothers watched their father's sheep graze in the country, Joseph visited them. When they saw Joseph coming, they seized their opportunity to retaliate for Joseph's humiliating dreams. At first they were going to kill him, but Reuben insisted they let him live. All didn't go according to Reuben's plan, however, and the other brothers sold Joseph to some merchants who were traveling to Egypt. As a result of his brothers' vindictive nature, Joseph disappeared from his family and his country and was sold in Egypt to a man named Potiphar to be a servant in his household.

Joseph may not have been in control of his destiny at the time, but he was not alone in his exile. God's Spirit was with him. God had a plan for Joseph's life, and the Spirit gifted Joseph with a special talent even when he was in a strange place. Although Joseph was a faithful and conscientious worker for Potiphar, he encountered a problem. Potiphar's wife was a conniving and devious woman who forced herself on Joseph, trying to get him to have sex with her. When he resisted her advances and ran from the house, she lied about the event to her husband, and Joseph ended up in prison.

While Joseph was confined, God's Spirit transformed him, the dreamer of future things, into the teller of dreams and their meanings. One day two men who served Pharaoh were put in the same prison as Joseph. One man had been the king's cupbearer, who made sure everything the king drank was pure. The other one had baked the king's bread. Late one night both men had dreams. When Joseph saw them the next morning, he asked them, "What's the matter? You both look upset."

"We had terrible dreams last night," the cupbearer and the baker told him. "We know these dreams mean something, but there's no one around to explain them to us."

"God is the only one who reveals the meaning of dreams," Joseph told them, "but maybe I can help. First you have to describe the entire dream to me."

The cupbearer spoke first. "I saw a large grapevine with three branches laden with large clusters of grapes. I picked the best ripe grapes and squeezed the juice directly into Pharaoh's cup. Then I brought the fresh-squeezed grape juice to him."

"Here's what your dream means," Joseph said. "In three days Pharaoh will call you back to the palace, and you'll provide him with whatever he needs to drink. All will return to normal for you, but if you have the opportunity, please mention me to Pharaoh. Tell him what I did for you, and maybe he'll let me out of prison."

The baker was excited about Joseph's favorable interpretation of the cupbearer's dream, so he eagerly recollected his own dream. "I had three baskets balanced on my head. The top one was filled with bread, biscuits, and sweet rolls for the king. Suddenly a flock of birds swooped down, settled on the baked goods, and started eating them."

Immediately Joseph knew what the baker's dream meant. Although it troubled him, he stated the truth: "In three days Pharaoh will summon you and release you from prison. But then he will put you to death and leave your body exposed. The birds will peck at your remains as they pecked at the bread in your dream."

In three days everything happened just as Joseph had said. The baker was executed, and the cupbearer returned to the service of the king.

Two long years passed, and Joseph remained incarcerated. Then one night Pharaoh had two terrifying dreams that scared him awake. By morning Pharaoh had riled up the entire royal household, frantic over his desire to know the meanings of his dreams. He called for all the magicians and wise men in his kingdom, but no one was crafty or skilled or wise enough to tell him what the dreams meant. Pharaoh was livid: "I am the king of the greatest kingdom in all the world, isn't there someone who is wise enough to interpret my dreams?"

Overhearing the king's ranting, the cupbearer recalled the prisoner named Joseph who had told him the meaning of his own dream years before. The cupbearer approached the king. "O great king," he said carefully, "there is someone who *is* wise enough to tell you the meaning of your dream—a Hebrew slave who remains in prison. I met him years ago when I was imprisoned for a time. He told me the meaning of my dream, which was fulfilled as he said. I'm sure he can do the same for you."

So the king ordered one of his assistants to release Joseph from prison and escort him to the palace. When Joseph stood in front of the royal throne, Pharaoh said, "I hear you can interpret dreams."

"I can't interpret dreams, O great king, but God

can," Joseph replied. "Only God knows the meaning of dreams. His Spirit is with me and will speak through me to tell you what your dreams mean."

Then Pharaoh described what he had dreamed. "I was standing at the Nile River, and I saw seven healthy cows grazing among the reeds. They were fat and sleek, the best cows I've ever seen. Then seven ugly, skinny cows came out of the water and gobbled up the fat cows. But even after eating those fat ones, the skinny cows stayed skinny.

"Then I had another dream. This time I saw seven heads of grain growing that were full and beautiful. Suddenly another seven heads of grain sprouted. They were scrawny and dried out from the wind. They jumped up and swallowed the good, healthy heads of grain, but they stayed thin. I've asked every magician and all the wise men in my kingdom what these images mean. But they are all too stupid to tell me."

"The two dreams are the same," Joseph told him. "God is telling you what he is going to do in the future. The seven fat cows and seven good heads of grain are seven years of great harvests. For seven years in a row there will be an abundance of food. You'll have so much grain and fruit you won't know where to store it all. The seven skinny cows and the seven brittle heads of grain represent seven years of no harvest, extreme drought, and famine. For seven years the rains won't come, the ground will be dry, and the grain and fruit won't grow. God gave you two similar dreams for a reason. He told you this twice, so it certainly will happen, and it's going to happen soon.

"Now here's what you need to do to get ready. Find someone to put in charge of the land of Egypt. During the first seven years, when the crops come in fat and full and there's lots of grain and corn, save part of each year's harvest and store it in barns so your country will have plenty of grain during the seven years when the crops barely grow. This famine will be severe not only in Egypt but throughout the world."

> So Pharaoh asked them, "Can we find anyone like this man, one in whom is the spirit of God?"
> (Genesis 41:38)

Pharaoh paused to consider his options, then said, "I choose you, Joseph. You're wiser than anyone in my kingdom. You'll be my second in command of Egypt because you have the Spirit of God in you."

So Joseph, once the favorite of his father, became the favorite of Pharaoh. And God's Spirit was with Joseph, giving him the wisdom and charisma to oversee Egypt's food supply.

Now things happened as the Spirit had revealed in

the dreams. After seven years of abundant harvest, nothing grew in the fields, not in Egypt or in the land of Canaan where Joseph's family lived. So in order to prevent themselves from starving, Joseph's father, his brothers, their wives, and their children moved to Egypt at the invitation of Pharaoh. They settled in the area of Goshen in Egypt, and their family lived there for hundreds of years.

The Spirit Today

Interpreting dreams is not exactly what we think of as a gift of the Spirit today; however, the Bible makes it clear that both wisdom and knowledge are provided through the Spirit (1 Cor. 12:8). During the time Joseph was in Egypt, God was with Joseph, providing him with the ability to discern the meaning of dreams. Joseph did not take the credit for his accomplishment; rather he openly stated the source of his ability, saying that only God could discern the meaning of dreams (Gen. 41:16). God chose Joseph to represent him to the Egyptians, and the Spirit supplied him with the special skills to fulfill his calling. Today God does the same—he chooses people to speak on his behalf, to preach, to teach, to write, to listen, and to do a wide variety of other tasks within the kingdom. He not only calls us, he equips us as well. Through his Spirit we received the appropriate and necessary abilities to complete the task at hand. The next time you hear of an opportunity to serve others, don't hide and excuse yourself with, "I can't do that, somebody else would be better." Step up and say yes and see how the Spirit will provide you with the ability to do God's work.

—

The Artistic Spirit Inspires a Craftsman

from Exodus 31:2–6, 35:30–35

After escaping the clutches of slavery in Egypt and crossing the Red Sea on dry ground, God's people traveled through the Sinai Peninsula until they reached the desert of Sinai, where they camped in front of the mountain. On top of Mount Sinai, God spoke to Moses, giving him the Ten Commandments and other laws for his people to live by. Desiring to be in a relationship with his people, God instructed them to "Be holy, for I am holy," and provided them with a set of standards for living holy lives. God also conveyed to Moses detailed instructions for assembling a special tent called a Tabernacle that would remind the people that God's presence was with them. Once constructed, the Tabernacle would be located in the middle of the camp, surrounded by the tribes of Israel and filled with God's glory. After spending forty days and nights on the mountain, Moses knew everything he needed to know about the Tabernacle: what materials to use, how to build it, how to care for it, and how to carry it from place to place. However, he still had one question for God: "Who's going to do this? Who's skilled enough to do all this elaborate work?" Moses asked God.

"Do you know Bezalel?" God asked Moses.

"Yes," Moses answered. "He's from the tribe of Judah, a skilled craftsman who shapes beautiful objects from gold and silver. He worked for Pharaoh while we lived in Egypt, and everything he made delighted him."

"That's the man," God replied. "Bezalel is indeed highly skilled and able to craft many things. But I will send him my Spirit, who will empower Bezalel to do extraordinary work. Everything he crafts for my Tabernacle will reflect my glory."

> Then Moses said to the Israelites, "See, the LORD has chosen Bezalel, son of Uri, the son of Hur, of the tribe of Judah, and he has filled him with the Spirit of God, with wisdom, with understanding, with knowledge and with all kinds of skills." (Exodus 35:30–31)

Later it happened just as God had said. God's Spirit infused Bezalel with the ability to design and build pieces of furniture and craft objects worthy of placement in God's holy tent. The Spirit came upon Bezalel without his knowledge, making him work with increased confidence as he cut and set gemstones, carved wood, wove fabrics, and molded gold, silver, and bronze into pieces of art. Another craftsman, Oholiab, was Bezalel's right-hand man. Together they gathered all the craftsmen of Israel, sharing with them the plans and detailed instructions God had provided.

With skill and confidence from the Spirit of God, Bezalel and his helpers carved the furniture out of wood and covered it with gold. He wove the fabrics for the priests' clothing from blue, purple, and scarlet yarn. He melted down gold and shaped it into a lamp stand. Bezalel carved a special chest called the Ark of the Covenant from acacia wood that would never rot. Then he covered the Ark with thin pieces of gold and made two gold cherubim to display on the lid. Other craftsmen wove fabric for the tent curtains and embroidered them with colorful thread. They formed the metal poles and rings that would hold up the tent, including every detail God had given Moses.

Bezalel needed the power of the Spirit within him to accomplish this holy and sacred task of crafting items that would signify the presence of Almighty God. No humans could do this on their own; only through the Spirit's power and guidance could this holy assignment be completed.

The Spirit Today

The Spirit lives in all of us, providing us with the breath of life and our very existence, as well as our various talents and abilities. The craftsmen who designed and artistically fashioned God's Tabernacle, the furniture and the fixtures, were specifically selected by God. They were skilled tradesmen, having already proven themselves in the service of the king of Egypt, but now they were called to work on the house of God that would display his glory and contain his presence. They needed Spirit-infused ability to accomplish these tasks.

No matter what our talent or ability, as we use it for God and to further his kingdom here on earth, the Spirit will be at work in and through us.

―

The Spirit Empowers Israel's Leaders

from Numbers 11:16–30

On the day the Israelites set up the Tabernacle and arranged the furniture in the assigned places, the great cloud of God moved into place over the Tabernacle, God's new dwelling place. During the day the cloud was bright white, and at night it glowed like fire, constantly reminding the people that God was with them, living right in the center of their camp.

A few weeks after the Tabernacle was finished, the cloud of God rose into the air and started to move. Knowing what the cloud's movement signified, Moses told the people, "It's time to pack up and move forward toward the land God has promised will become ours." So the Israelites took down their tents, packed up their possessions, gathered their children, and arranged themselves in groups to leave the camp at Mount Sinai in an orderly fashion, according to the arrangement God had given Moses. They walked in the wilderness for three days, following the cloud of God. When the cloud stopped in the Desert of Paran, the Israelites stopped. The men in charge of the Tabernacle pitched the tent for the house of God. Then every tribe and family of Israel set up their tents around the Tabernacle in the exact way that God had instructed.

Days passed, and the people settled into their usual routine. Each morning they gathered manna, God's bread from heaven that he had provided for his people while they lived in the desert. Then one day someone in the camp said, "Does anyone remember the food we had in Egypt? Do you remember the taste of fresh fish sautéed with leeks, garlic, and onions?"

"Oh, yes, indeed I do," said another. "As well as the crunchy cucumbers and ripe, juicy watermelons!"

"How I wish I had some vegetables or lamb instead of this tasteless manna. My stomach is full, but I want the taste of something different," someone else added.

Soon everyone in the camp was yearning for the food they had consumed in Egypt. They complained. They wailed. They whined to Moses. Groups chanted, "We want meat. We want meat. We want meat!" The loud wailing and chanting of a thousand voices made Moses' ears ring with noise late into the night.

"What am I going to do with all these grumbling people?" Moses asked God. "Why did you make *me* responsible for all of them? They keep whining and moaning that they want meat to eat. Where could I get enough meat to feed two million people? They're making me tired. I'm so exhausted I want to die and be free of them."

> The LORD said to Moses: "Bring me seventy of Israel's elders....I will take some of the power of the Spirit that is on you and put it on them." (Numbers 11:16, 17)

"Moses, listen to me," God said. "You don't have to do this alone. I'll take care of the demand for meat. In fact, the people will have more than enough meat to eat for a month. But here's what *you* need to do first. Find the best leaders in Israel and tell them to meet you at the Tabernacle, where I will take my Spirit that is on you and put my Spirit in each of them. Then they will be equipped to share the leadership responsibilities with you. You won't have to lead my people alone anymore."

Immediately Moses issued an order through the

camp for seventy men to help him. When the wisest and best leaders of the camp gathered, they circled the Tabernacle and waited in silence. Then God descended from the cloud that hovered over the Tabernacle and spoke to Moses. As he had explained to Moses, God took some of his Spirit that was in Moses and placed it in the hearts and minds of the other leaders. The Leader-Making Spirit filled them with his power, giving them wisdom, confidence, and charisma to lead God's great nation.

The seventy newly Spirit-filled men were jubilant. They sang and danced and praised God, demonstrating to all the people of Israel that God's Spirit lived not only in Moses but in them as well.

Most of the leaders had followed Moses' instructions and had grouped together at the Tabernacle, but two hadn't bothered to join them. Eldad and Medad were off by themselves when God spread his Spirit out through the group of recruits. The alternate location of the two, however, didn't matter to God's Spirit, who rested on them as he did the others. This inconsistency, however, was unsettling to those who watched. When Joshua was made aware of the disobedient behavior, he ran to Moses and said, "We need to stop these men! They didn't follow your instructions."

But Moses was not alarmed. "Don't worry, Joshua," Moses replied calmly. "You don't have to stand up for me. I'm not concerned at all about sharing God's Spirit. Indeed, I wish the Lord would put his Spirit on all people."

Someday the Spirit would come and fill all believers just as Moses wished. Someday the Spirit's power would come, not just for a moment to handle a situation, not just to respond to an emergency or for a special purpose, but to stay forever in the hearts and minds of all believers, transforming their lives and developing their characters.

The Spirit Today

Joshua, a military leader of God's people, expected people to follow orders and do what was required of them. It's no surprise then that he was alarmed when Eldad and Medad didn't show up in the right place. In Joshua's eyes, disobeying orders wasn't acceptable, and he pointed it out to Moses. Moses, however, was not concerned; he knew that the Spirit finds those he chooses, regardless of place or time.

Sometimes we find ourselves thinking like Joshua as we lose sight of the bigger picture and obsess over irrelevant details. We may think that the Spirit should come only on those who follow the rules, do things a certain way, or are worthy of the Spirit's gifts. We may even be judgmental about someone's display of the gift the Spirit has given them. Our perception may be too restrictive. God sees things differently than we do—he wants to pour out his Spirit abundantly on all people. There is plenty to go around.

~

The Spirit Speaks through an Outsider

from Numbers 22–24

The Israelites spent many years wandering around in the desert, learning to trust God. As they neared the end of their journey and approached the region of Canaan, they first had to travel through the country of Moab.

Now Balak, the king of Moab, was more than a little concerned about two million people tromping across his territory. He had heard stories about the Israelites and was afraid they would mow down his crops, steal the sheep and cattle, and destroy anything in their path. So he did what he always did:

he decided to put a curse on the invaders to thwart their progress, through the greatest sorcerer in the region—Balaam, who lived in Aram, more than one hundred miles north of Moab.

"I'll have Balaam come and curse this mob of people so they won't be able to fight against me," the king reasoned. "I'll send my best princes to impress him, and I'll offer him so much money he won't refuse my request."

So the princes from Moab traveled to Aram and presented the king's letter to Balaam. Balaam, however, wasn't impressed with the princes and demanded more money. Then he sent the princes away. So the king of Moab sent another group of princes to Balaam, who promised him even more money. This time Balaam agreed to travel to Moab and curse the Israelites for the king in exchange for a substantial payment.

Balaam mounted his donkey and started on the long journey. God, however, was not pleased. He disapproved of Balaam's plan to curse his people, so God sent an angel to stop Balaam. After many miles of walking, Balaam's donkey saw an angel standing in the middle of the road holding a large sword in his hand. To avoid the flashing sword, the donkey strayed off the road and entered a nearby field. Balaam, who couldn't see the angel in the road, screamed at his donkey, "Get back on the road, you stupid animal." He hit the donkey with a stick, and they continued their journey.

After a while Balaam and the donkey came to a narrow path between the walls of two vineyards. Suddenly the angel appeared again to the donkey. Trying to pass by the angel, the donkey squeezed up against one of the walls and squashed Balaam's foot in the process. Unaware of the angel's presence, Balaam screamed, "What are you doing, you stupid donkey!" and struck the donkey again.

Later they came to a narrow spot in the road, and the angel suddenly appeared a third time. The donkey couldn't move to the right or to the left to avoid the angel, so he just lay down, right there in the middle of the road. Balaam, oblivious to the obstacle, was furious and smacked the donkey with his stick. Then God opened the donkey's mouth and made her say, "What have I done to make you beat me?"

"You've made me look foolish and silly," Balaam replied.

"But I've been a good donkey to you all these years. Have I ever done this before?"

"No, you haven't. You've been a good donkey," replied Balaam, not even realizing he was addressing a talking donkey!

Then God opened Balaam's eyes, and he saw the angel. "Three times I blocked the path so you wouldn't continue the journey," the angel said. "Your donkey saw me and turned off the road to save you from my sword."

"I'm sorry. If you still think this trip is evil, I'll go back home," said Balaam.

"You may continue on to Moab," said the angel. "But you must utter only the words God's Spirit tells you to say."

When King Balak received news that the princes and Balaam were approaching the border of Moab, he mounted his horse and rode out to meet the sorcerer. Balak, angry about the delay, shouted at Balaam, "Why did you take so long to get here? Didn't I send you an urgent message? Didn't I promise you enough money to come right away?"

"Well," said Balaam calmly, "I'm here now. But I'm warning you, I'll only tell you what the Spirit wants me to say. The words will be his, not mine."

When Balaam looked out and saw Israel encamped tribe by tribe, the Spirit of God came on him and he spoke his message. (Numbers 24:2–3)

The next morning Balak took Balaam to a mountain peak overlooking the Israelite camp. They viewed the nation of two million people spread out in the valley below. Then the Spirit of God came beside Balaam, and as Balaam opened his mouth to speak, the Spirit provided these words: "How can I say bad things about the people God loves? They are like specks of dust, there's too many of them to count."

"That's not what I wanted to hear you say," King Balak shouted. "Maybe you'll say something different from a different location. Let's go someplace else."

King Balak and Balaam moved to another place on the cliff. God's Spirit again filled Balaam's mouth with words. "Listen, Balak," Balaam said. "God is not like people. He doesn't tell lies, he doesn't change his mind. When he says something, he does it. When he makes a promise, he keeps it. He has promised good things to his people. He has blessed them, and there's no way I can undo God's blessing. No magic can harm them. Nobody can hurt them."

King Balak was furious. His face turned beet red, and he stomped his feet, clapped his hands, and shouted, "That's terrible news! I didn't ask you to tell me *that*! I'm not paying you for information! I want you to curse these people or predict bad things will happen to them so they won't attack me. I'd be pleased if you just made them go away. But all you've done is say good things about them."

"Well," said Balaam, "I can only say the things that God's Spirit tells me to say. I told you that from the beginning. I'm not really talking, God's Spirit is talking through me."

"Get out of here!" the king screamed. "I would have paid you lots of money, but you didn't do what I asked. Go home."

"I came because you offered me a lot of money, but I have no control over what I say," Balaam explained. "Even if you gave me enough gold and silver to fill every room in your palace, I could not say bad things against the people of God. I could not disobey God. I can only say what his Spirit tells me. Someday a star will come from their ancestor Jacob, and a scepter will rise out of Israel. He will rule over all the nations, and Israel will become wealthy."

Still furious, the king of Moab left the mountain, disgruntled and dissatisfied. And Balaam, even though he had seen the power and control of God's Spirit, was upset because he hadn't gotten his money after all.

The Spirit Today

The continuous struggles between good and evil, blessings and curses in the world are clearly evident in this story. As a sorcerer, Balaam thought he could overpower good and bring about evil through a curse on God's people. He obviously had no idea whom he was dealing with. God used the power of the Spirit to protect and defend his people from evil. Today the Spirit keeps us from evil and protects us from the Evil One and from the powers of darkness. "For the Spirit God gave us does not make us timid, but gives us power, love and self-discipline" (2 Tim. 1:7). We are never left to fend for ourselves on our own; the Spirit equips us to stand strong against the powers of evil and of Satan (Eph. 6:10–17).

Chapter Three

The Spirit Moves People to Action

"If the Holy Spirit moves, nothing can stop him."

Francis Chan

As God's people were on the border of Canaan, they needed the power of the Spirit more than ever to help them take over the Promised Land. Under the Spirit's power, Moses' replacement Joshua led the people into Canaan. The Spirit-filled Joshua led with boldness and courage to execute God's plan for his people. As the people settled in the land, they experienced a time of peace and rest—another blessing from the Spirit.

Unfortunately, as time passed, the Israelites adopted the practices of their neighbors, blending in with their cultural ways and worship of idols rather than remaining a separate and holy people for God. Their peace and rest were shattered as God sent strife and conflict from local and foreign invaders to make them realize their tragic mistake of forgetting him. When they pleaded with God for his help, he sent deliverance through a string of people called judges. These people were insignificant or weak on their own, but exemplary and bold under the Spirit's power. As Israel settled down, its people eventually desired a monarchy rather than a theocracy, which God allowed. The Spirit moved the leaders of God's people to action, to charge into battle, cleverly humiliate the enemy, become a king, speak up, write poetry, or create a temple for God. Through the Spirit's power, ordinary people were equipped to accomplish the tasks God had appointed them to do.

The Spirit Empowers Joshua to Lead God's Nation

from Numbers 27:12–23

Moses, the great leader of God's people, was getting older than old. He was 120 when the Israelites reached the border of the land God had promised them. Then God came to Moses and said, "My Spirit has been with you the entire time you have been the leader of my people. Joshua also has my Spirit. He will be the next great leader of my people. He will bring my people into the Promised Land."

Looking back, Moses realized that God's Spirit had been with Joshua for a long, long time. When the Amalekites attacked the Israelites in the desert, the Spirit had given Joshua military strength, courage, and knowledge to lead the army into battle. When Joshua was selected to be one of the spies to check out the land of Canaan, the Spirit had helped him believe that the Israelites could conquer the people who lived there. When Moses needed more leaders to help him, God's Spirit had filled Joshua with the wisdom to be one of the seventy leaders of God's people. Joshua's leadership skills were not his own—they came from God's Spirit living in him.

So the LORD said to Moses, "Take Joshua son of Nun, a man in whom is the spirit of leadership, and lay your hand on him.... Give him some of your authority so the whole Israelite community will obey him." (Numbers 27:18, 20)

So Moses called the people together. In front of all of them and the priest Eleazar, he placed his hands on Joshua. Then he addressed the audience: "God has chosen Joshua to be your next leader after I am gone. God's Spirit is with him. Eleazar the priest will also help him decide what God wants him to do. You must follow his command into battle and back again. Listen to him, for God's Spirit is with him as it was with me."

Joshua was now equipped to lead God's people into the Promised Land. After their forty-year journey from Egypt, the Israelites were ready for their dream to come true. Joshua would help them settle down in the land flowing with milk and honey, and God's Spirit would be with them so they would live in peace.

Like cattle that go down to the plain, [the Israelites] were given rest by the Spirit of the LORD. (Isaiah 63:14)

The Spirit Today

Joshua was the perfect candidate to be Moses' successor as the leader of Israel. He'd had years of preparation as Moses' assistant (Exod. 24:13; Num. 11:28), as a military leader (Exod. 17:8–13), and as a faithful and trustworthy scout of the new land (Num. 13–14). His training had been thorough, and he was well known among the people. He was one of only three men who had been with God's people every step of the journey since they had left Egypt. Although his qualifications were exemplary, he had something that far exceeded his training: Joshua had God's Spirit.

The Spirit has always been and continues to be in the leader-equipping business. He calls, commissions, and equips leaders to God's service. When he calls us to serve God in various ways and in various areas of life, he calls us to perform God's work here on earth. The Spirit is with us to use our experiences, provide training, and support us in God's work.

The Spirit Turns Gideon into a Brave Warrior

from Judges 6–7

Trouble was brewing in Canaan. The wandering herdsmen from Midian had invaded the Israelites' land and were terrorizing the people. The Midianites, migrating from the south, stormed through the fields on their camels, trampling the grain. Their herds of cattle consumed the crops, and their tents sprang up overnight in the fields like mushrooms after a spring rain. The invaders snatched the Israelites' sheep, cattle, and donkeys, and frightened the Israelites, forcing them to flee to the mountains and live in caves. Meanwhile, in the valleys below, the Midianites enjoyed the goodness of the land God had intended for his people.

The Israelites were miserable, poor, and hungry, so they cried to God and begged him for deliverance. One of the Israelites in hiding, named Gideon, was from a small clan in the tribe of Manasseh. He was threshing his grain in a winepress rather than in the open fields, as he was afraid of the Midianites stealing the little grain he had.

While Gideon worked, an angel of the Lord suddenly appeared in front of him. "Gideon," he said, "God has chosen you, of all the people in Israel, to fight the Midianites and chase them out of your country."

Then the Spirit of the LORD came on Gideon, and he blew a trumpet, summoning the Abiezrites to follow him. (Judges 6:34)

Then God's Spirit came upon Gideon like a thunderbolt. The power of the Spirit spread through him, and he was no longer afraid. He stopped threshing the grain and bravely ventured into the open countryside. Gideon blew a ram's horn whose blast echoed through the valleys, signaling to the young men of Israel to unite for battle under their new leader. They came running from all directions, eager to fight the Midianites and win back the land. In a short time Gideon had an army of thirty-two thousand soldiers!

In the morning God said to Gideon, "There are too many men. If any of them are afraid to fight, tell them to go back home." So Gideon gathered the troops and announced, "If you're afraid to fight, you're free to go back home." Twenty-two thousand soldiers left the camp and returned to their hometowns. Then the army had ten thousand men—still a very large number.

God talked to Gideon again. "There are still too many men. Take them down to the brook. If they kneel down and lap up the water from the stream like a dog, send them home. But keep those who scoop up the water with their hands." Gideon followed God's directions, dismissing the men who knelt down to lap the water. Now his army was whittled down to just three hundred soldiers.

Meanwhile the Midianite army congregated in the valley with its hordes of camels, equipment, and tents. Gideon's meager group of three hundred men assembled on the ridge, prepared to challenge this powerful force. Most military leaders would assume this was a suicidal mission, but Gideon had a secret weapon—the Spirit of God. He knew that the Spirit's power would triumph over human strength, over fast-footed animals, and over the best weapons of war.

In the middle of the night, Gideon said to the troops, "Get up! Tonight the Lord will win this battle for us." Then Gideon divided the men into three groups and handed each man a ram's horn and an empty jar with a burning torch inside. "Watch me and follow my lead," he said. "When I approach the camp and blow my trumpet, blow yours as loud as you can and shout, 'For the Lord and for Gideon!'"

Gideon's army marched into the hills surrounding the valley where the Midianite army was sleeping. In the darkness Gideon blew his trumpet. The three hundred men followed his lead: they blew their trumpets, smashed their jars, and lifted their burning torches high. They shouted together at the top of their lungs, "For the Lord and for Gideon!" Then they stood still and watched. Their shouts shook the hillsides and echoed in the valley. The sound of smashing pottery and shouting terrorized the Midianites, who woke up totally confused. In the dark the warriors grabbed their swords and started swinging, killing one another. They fled from the valley and retreated to their own country. Through God's Spirit, Gideon had had the ability to lead the army to victory.

The Spirit Today

Many of us can relate to Gideon—he was timid, he was fearful of what was going on around him, and he made excuses for why he could not lead (Judg. 6:15). Then as now, God calls people to service. He will have nothing to do with our excuses; he will, however, patiently handle our questions and allow us to process our doubts and fears. Then he moves us forward, eliminating obstacles and readying us to serve. We need to listen to his instructions and obediently follow, trusting that the Spirit will fill in the holes and gaps in our lives, shore up our limitations, and strengthen us to do God's work.

—

The Spirit Transforms Saul into a King

from I Samuel 10, I Samuel 11:1–13

For hundreds of years the judges had led the Israelites through the power of the Spirit, but the people of Israel were dissatisfied with their leadership structure. They wanted to be more like the countries around them. They wanted a king.

The last judge, Samuel, tried to reason with the people, "You already have the greatest king of all, the King of Glory, the Lord Almighty. He is your Ruler. He is your King." But the people disagreed with him. They wanted a *real* king they could see, a human king—a king who would lead them into battle and protect them with an army. A king who wore a crown and fancy robes. A king who lived in a palace and drove a chariot. They wanted to hear a kingly voice assuring them that all was well. Perplexed and disappointed in the people, Samuel prayed to God, seeking his guidance, and received God's reply: "Do what they want, Samuel. Give them a king. When the time is right, I will show you whom I've chosen."

Not long after that, God said to Samuel, "Someone from the tribe of Benjamin will be coming to see you. He's the one I've chosen to be Israel's king, so anoint him with oil to indicate that the people have a new leader."

The next day, as God had foretold, a man named Saul arrived in the town. He approached the first person he saw (who happened to be Samuel) and said, "My father's donkeys have wandered away and I'm looking for someone who can help me locate them."

"I can help you," Samuel replied. "Stay here and we'll have supper together. Don't worry about the donkeys, someone else found them. But I'll tell you something special—you and your family will bring hope to the nation of Israel."

"How can that happen?" Saul asked. "My family isn't important, and I'm from the tribe of Benjamin—the smallest tribe in Israel. We're a group of nobodies."

Samuel didn't comment. Instead, he threw a big feast for thirty guests, with Saul and his servants as guests of honor. During dinner he gave Saul the best pieces of meat, signifying he was someone special. After dinner Samuel took Saul off to a special place to worship God.

[Samuel said to Saul,] "The Spirit of the LORD will come powerfully upon you, and you will prophesy with them; and you will be changed into a different person. Once these signs are fulfilled, do whatever your hand finds to do, for God is with you." (I Samuel 10:6–7)

The next morning, as Saul was about to leave, Samuel stopped him. "Don't go yet," he said. "I have a special message from God for you." Then Samuel poured the sacred anointing oil over Saul's head and kissed him. "I'm doing this because God has chosen you to be king over Israel," Samuel explained. "God will send you three signs on your way home to assure you he wants you as king. First: you'll meet two men who'll tell you the donkeys were found and your father is looking for you. Second: near the oak tree in Tabor you'll meet three men with three goats, three loaves of bread, and a wineskin full of wine. They'll offer you two loaves of bread. Take them. Third: at Gibeah you'll meet prophets playing a harp, a tambourine, a flute, and a lyre. After all this happens, do what you have to do; God will be with you."

As Saul left the town, God changed his attitude and thinking. Then the events Samuel had predicted occurred. First two men told Saul his father was looking for him. When Saul came to the oak tree he saw the three men with the goats, bread, and wine. And when he came to Gibeah, the group of prophets appeared just as Samuel had said. They were playing their instruments and praising God. They jumped and leaped and danced in the street, full of joy. Then, in a forceful rush, God's Spirit seized Saul and filled him with joy. He joined the group of prophets, singing and dancing as wildly as they were. Saul had never behaved like this before, but God's Spirit was making an announcement: "This man is special to me. I have chosen him to lead my people."

Only a few people knew God had chosen Saul to lead the Israelites, so after a while Samuel called the people together to present Saul as their new king. When everyone was assembled, they looked at each other and said, "So where's Saul?" No one could find him. Finally Samuel asked God for some guidance, and God informed him, "Saul is hiding. You'll find him in the piles of baggage."

When Saul stood up from his hiding place, his impressive height was evident; he was much taller than the rest of the people. He was a good-looking young man—the best-looking guy in all of Israel. Besides that, he was from a wealthy and powerful family. Immediately the people realized Saul was the kingly type of person they so desired, so they declared their allegiance to him by shouting, "Long live the king! Long live the king!"

And that was the end of the ceremony. No party, no special parade, no crown or royal red robe. No white horse, no queen or princesses, no stately palace, no padded velvet throne. In fact, the new king went back home to work in the fields. And everybody else went home too.

But serious trouble was brewing that would require the king's attention. The Ammonites were bullying God's people in the city of Jabesh, threatening to gouge out their eyes. In panic the people of Jabesh sent a message to the new king, begging for his help. When the people in Saul's hometown of Gibeah heard the horrible news, they were furious and broke down in grief and fear.

Having plowed his fields all day, Saul was on his way home with his oxen when he saw the crying group of people. "What's wrong?" Saul asked the wailing group. "The Ammonites have threatened to humiliate the men of Jabesh and cut out their right eyes!" the people replied. "If no one helps them, the Ammonites will do what they said."

As the men finished their announcement, God's Spirit forcefully grabbed hold of Saul and filled him with power and determination. Saul was furious, but his anger moved him to action. Through the Spirit's power Saul knew what to do to save God's people from the Ammonites. He killed his oxen, butchered them into pieces, and handed out the hunks of raw meat to his men.

"Take these pieces to the twelve tribes of Israel," he commanded. "As you hand out the meat, give the people this message: Saul will do the same to your oxen if you don't follow him and Samuel into battle against the Ammonites."

When Saul heard their words, the Spirit of God came powerfully upon him, and he burned with anger. (I Samuel 11:6)

Saul's plan worked. Men from every corner of Israel gathered together as one army to fight the Ammonites. The army of 330,000 men followed Saul, who was filled with God's Spirit, into battle. They attacked in the middle of the night and fought until the middle of the next day. When the battle was over, Saul knew God had made the victory possible.

He stood before the people and shouted, "Today the Lord has brought salvation to Israel. Today he has rescued his people!"

The Spirit Today

The pouring of sacred oil over the chosen king's head symbolized the pouring out of the Spirit's power and presence on the king, making him a servant of God to the people. This holy process reminded the king that his power, position, and authority were ordained by God and not of his own doing, and that he should lead with God's wisdom and not his own. The Spirit qualified Saul for his official function as king; when Saul no longer served in that official capacity, the power of the Spirit was no longer required.

Most of us will never be anointed with sacred oil for our work, but we are still called to it by God, and the Spirit provides us with talent to fulfill that calling. Our greatest success will come when we allow the Spirit to work through us and our weaknesses to display God's power working through our life.

The Spirit Empowers Young David as King

from I Samuel 16:1–13

King Saul eventually disobeyed God and broke his laws; as a result, God regretted that he had made Saul king. God selected another person to be king—someone who already loved him.

God told Samuel, "Go to Bethlehem and find a man named Jesse. I have chosen one of his sons to be king."

Samuel traveled to the town of Bethlehem and met with Jesse and his sons. As soon as Samuel saw the oldest boy, Eliab, he thought, "This must be the one. He's tall and handsome." But God told him, "Don't just look at his appearance. People judge others by their looks, but I judge a person by what's inside. He's not the one to be king."

Then Samuel met another son, Abinadab. And Samuel said, "God hasn't chosen him either." The next son, Shammah, came to meet Samuel, but Samuel said, "He's not the one." One by one Jesse's sons met Samuel. And each time Samuel knew that God hadn't selected that son to be king.

Finally Samuel asked Jesse, "Do you have any other boys?"

"Yes," Jesse said reluctantly. "There's one more, my youngest son. He's out in the fields taking care of the sheep." But he was really thinking, "It can't be David. He's too young, he's too short, he has absolutely no experience to be a king." But Jesse kept quiet.

"Someone go find him and bring him to me," Samuel instructed. "I have time to wait for him to come here."

One of Jesse's older boys ran out to the fields and returned with his little brother. As soon as Samuel saw the young shepherd boy, he heard God whisper, "That's whom I've chosen. This is the one you must anoint as king. He will be the next king of Israel."

> So Samuel took the horn of oil and anointed him in the presence of his brothers, and from that day on the Spirit of the LORD came powerfully upon David. (1 Samuel 16:13)

No one thought the young boy named David was ready to be a king; after all, he knew only how to protect and care for sheep, not a nation of people. Following Samuel's lead, however, Jesse and the older brothers circled around young David. Then Samuel raised the horn of olive oil up high and poured the sacred oil over David's head. As the oil ran down David's hair and over his ears, the Spirit settled on David. He wrapped himself around the boy like a cape and filled him with power. On his own, David wasn't equipped to be king, but now he had the power of the Spirit to give him courage, wisdom, and divine charisma to lead God's people.

Twice now Samuel had used the anointing oil as a symbol of the Spirit being poured on the one God had chosen as king. Someday God's Spirit would come without the symbol of oil. Someday God would approach his people; without the help of a priest, without the symbol of oil, he would directly and intimately pour out 100 percent of his Spirit on all his people.

The Spirit Today

David was filled with the Spirit at his anointing to be king. He was not instantly ready, however—he spent years learning, first in the royal courts and then out in the wilderness. He was filled with the Spirit, but his life was not easy. He had to dodge Saul's wrath and maneuver through human circumstances and court drama.

God's calling to do his work, and his provision of

the Spirit within our lives to fulfill that calling, is not a guarantee we will be free from conflict, struggle, and suffering as we navigate a sinful workplace and world. We are, however, assured of an inner peace in knowing that God's Spirit is with us.

―

The Spirit's Power Makes Amasai Bold

from 1 Chronicles 12:16–18

As the years passed, David became famous in Israel. First he killed the giant Goliath with his slingshot; then he led the Israelite army into several battles and won every time. The people of Israel thought he was a wonderful warrior and hero. As David became famous, King Saul became furious. He was jealous that the people liked David more than they liked him. Eventually Saul got so angry he tried to kill David, and David had to run for his life.

David lived as a fugitive in mountain caves and in enemy territory. He roamed the desert and wandered the countryside. His brothers and relatives were the first to join him; eventually other men sided with

David against Saul, until David was the leader of four hundred brave and skilled warriors. Some were experts in throwing long spears and blocking enemy arrows with their shields, others were skilled with a bow and arrow or a slingshot. Over time David attracted thousands of troops—an army of followers who wanted him to be king of Israel rather than King Saul.

One day thirty men from the tribes of Benjamin (which Saul was from) and Judah (which David was from) came to David in his hideout in the desert. They wanted to join David's army, but David wasn't sure he could trust them. When he saw them approaching his camp, David shouted to them, "If you came here in peace and plan to help me, then we can be friends. But if you came to spy on me to inform Saul of my whereabouts, then God will punish you."

Then the Spirit came on Amasai, chief of the Thirty. (1 Chronicles 12:18)

Amasai, the leader of the group, was not a skilled or eloquent speaker—not in front of common people, to say nothing of a future king. But the Spirit of God came on Amasai powerfully, turning a basic warrior into a confident and eloquent speaker, supplying him with a brief but convincing statement: "We're on your side, David. All of us want to fight for you. I wish you great success, prosperity, and peace so those who help you will also succeed. God is fighting for you because he's on your side."

With those words Amasai convinced David that these thirty mighty men sincerely desired to help him. As a result of that speech, David invited the men to join him and made them leaders of his troops. Once again the Spirit supplied the appropriate words and boldness to an available bystander.

The Spirit Today

Although the Bible shares scant information on Amasai's character, it provides the most important information—that the Spirit influenced him at a critical moment in his life. The basics of his life were typical of a Hebrew's of that day. He was a believer in the Almighty God of Israel, and had been raised to know God's law and commandments. He observed the appropriate feast days and performed the accepted rituals and offerings. But the task of speaking up bravely and boldly required a special infusion from the Spirit. From this story and the assurance that "the

Spirit helps us in our weakness" (Rom. 8:26) we can rely on the Spirit in our times of need. Even when we are filled with the Spirit, we will occasionally need his renewal—a boost of his power and presence, especially as we face challenging situations in our lives.

―

The Spirit Speaks through Poetry

from 2 Samuel 23, Psalm 51

> The Spirit of the LORD spoke through me. (2 Samuel 23:2)

When Samuel anointed David, God's Spirit moved out of King Saul and moved over to live in David. In those days God's Spirit filled a person and helped them for a short time, giving them the skill or ability to do what God had instructed them to do. But when the task was completed, the Spirit departed. God, however, promised his people that someday the Spirit would act differently. He would come and stay forever and fill the hearts of God's people. But that time was still in the future.

King David was concerned that God would take away his Spirit, since that's exactly what God had done with Saul. David knew Saul had disobeyed God, which had resulted in the Spirit's departure. David, certain of his own sins and disobedience, feared the Spirit would leave him as well, and wrote a special prayer to God:

> *Cleanse me with hyssop, and I will be clean;*
> *wash me, and I will be whiter than snow.*
> *Let me hear joy and gladness;*
> *let the bones you have crushed rejoice.*
> *Hide your face from my sins*
> *and blot out all my iniquity.*
>
> *Create in me a pure heart, O God,*
> *and renew a steadfast spirit within me.*
> *Do not cast me from your presence*
> *or take your Holy Spirit from me.*
>
> (Psalm 51:7–11)

God heard and answered David's prayer. God's Spirit had come to live in David as a young boy, giving David the ability to play the harp, write poetry, and compose songs of praise. The Spirit made David a brave warrior, successful in battle against God's enemies, and a great and wise king of Israel. The Spirit stayed with David, living in his heart, soul, and mind for all the years he was alive.

The Spirit Today

David beautifully expressed his greatest fear—that the Spirit would desert him as he had Saul. Sometimes we may have this same fear, since we know we are sinful and flawed like Saul. Saul's situation, however, was different from ours. The Spirit left him because he was no longer in the position of king. The Spirit had come to him for the express purpose of his kingship. In the Old Testament the Spirit's presence was typically temporary, given for a specific purpose and a specific time. We live in a different time and age: Jesus has come to earth, has sacrificed himself for us to free us from the consequences of sin. If we are Christian and believe in Jesus' salvation for us, the Spirit is in us. The Spirit continues living in us to renew us and sanctify us. We have these promises from God: "You, however, are not in the realm of the flesh but are in the realm of the Spirit, if indeed the Spirit of God lives in you.... For those who are led by the Spirit of God are the children of God" (Rom. 8:9, 14).

—

The Spirit Plans God's Temple through King David

from I Chronicles 28

When Israel was a new nation wandering in the desert, God's Spirit gave Israel's craftsmen special skills to build the Tabernacle. Hundreds of years later, God still resided in that tent while his people lived in homes made of wood. The nation's king even lived in a palace in the city of Jerusalem, while God resided in a tent in the town of Gibeon where the people gathered to worship.

The realization of this imbalance weighed heavy on the king, and caused him to envision a worthy house for God. King David presented an idea to Nathan, an adviser and prophet. "I'm living in a huge house made from cedar, but God still lives in a tent," David said. "This is all wrong. I need to build a house for God."

Although Nathan initially agreed with the king's reasoning, he received a message from God that changed his mind. During the night God spoke to

Nathan and told him, "Tell David he can't build a house for me. I've lived in the Tabernacle since it was constructed in the desert. I've never requested a permanent house. Besides, David isn't the right person to build a holy dwelling place. He's been a warrior his entire life and has caused too much bloodshed and death. After he dies I'll give Israel peace on every one of its borders by making one of David's sons king of Israel. That king will be a peaceful man, the perfect person to construct a temple where I will dwell."

The next morning, after Nathan informed David about God's plan, David returned to doing what he did best—conquering Israel's enemies and expanding the borders of the nation. To the west he fought and defeated the Philistines and took over their land along the Mediterranean Sea. Then he fought Israel's enemies to the east and captured the land as far as the Euphrates River. Everywhere David traveled with his army, God provided victory, until the boundaries of the kingdom were the exact ones God had promised to Abraham centuries before.

From the armies he defeated, David seized valuables. He acquired gold shields and iron chariots, large quantities of bronze, and articles of gold and silver from every nation he conquered. He saved everything to be used for the future Temple.

As King David aged, he no longer led his army into battle. He delegated this position to others while he stayed in Jerusalem. After retiring from the battle-field, David began to envision the plans for a beautiful Temple for God. In the quiet of the night the Spirit helped him imagine magnificent plans for God's house, a place more splendid than anything the world had ever seen. David chose Mount Moriah for the Temple's location—the highest peak in the city of Jerusalem. He envisioned the Temple gleaming in the sun high above everything else and visible from a dis-tance to anyone traveling to Jerusalem.

He made lists of the materials needed for the building and gathered the supplies: cedar logs from Sidon and Tyre, iron to make nails and gate hinges, huge quantities of gold for dishes and wall cover-ings, heaps of silver and mountains of bronze. Piles and piles of cedar logs mounted up, so many logs that no one could count them. He gathered skilled work-ers: stonecutters, carpenters, masons, wood-carvers, craftsmen, and artists.

Over the years, King David wrote and sketched out the plans and made lists of who would help and the supplies that would be needed. He counted the Levites and priests, assigning them special tasks for when the Temple was completed: some would present offerings to God on the altar, others would play instruments or sing in worship to the Lord; some would keep the Temple clean or bake the holy bread, and others would guard the treasures stored in the Temple storerooms or stand by the entrances to the Temple.

[David] gave [Solomon] the plans of all that the Spirit had put in his mind for the courts of the temple of the LORD and all the surrounding rooms, for the treasuries of the temple of God and for the treasuries for the dedicated things. (1 Chronicles 28:12)

When David had completed the plans for the Temple, he called all the leaders of the land together and held a meeting in Jerusalem. He stood in front of the people and said, "Listen to me, everyone. I had my heart set on building a Temple for the Lord. But God told me I had fought too many wars and had caused men to die and so I am not the proper person to build his sacred house. Instead he chose a man of peace, my son Solomon, to rule over Israel and build a house for him."

Then David turned to Solomon and said, "Here are the plans for the Temple. They were written for me by God's hand. His Spirit gave me all these details. This work is important because this place is not for a person but for the Lord God Almighty, King of the Universe. It must reveal the splendor of God and be famous. The nations of the world will talk about it in awe. God is in heaven, and this will be his footstool on earth. Don't be afraid. Be strong and courageous. The Lord God, my God, will be with you. Now do the work God has called you to do."

A few years later, Solomon and over 150,000 workmen started building God's Temple. They carefully followed the plans King David had envisioned and made the furniture, the decorations, and the dishes to his specifications. For seven years they labored in constructing the building and crafting the decorations. The completed Temple was large and astonishingly beautiful in every detail. At the dedication of the Temple, God's Spirit came to dwell in it. God's presence entered the Temple in the form of a cloud, filling the sanctuary with God's glory.

The Spirit Today

In the Old Testament the Spirit inspired the building of both the Tabernacle and the Temple, the holy places where God dwelled with his people. Today the

Spirit continues to inspire places in which God will dwell. They may not necessarily be physical structures; rather they can be those who collectively build the body of Christ, the church: "We are the temple of the living God" (2 Cor. 6:16). The work of the Spirit as a builder of God's dwelling places continues. "Don't you know that you yourselves are God's temple and that God's Spirit dwells in your midst?" (1 Cor. 3:16).

The Spirit Urges Azariah to Speak Up

from 2 Chronicles 15

After King David died, his son Solomon became king. But after Solomon died the Israelites couldn't agree on who should be the next king; consequently the nation divided into two, one nation called Israel, the other called Judah, each with its own king. After a succession of kings in each nation, a man named Asa became king of Judah. Overall Asa was a good king who loved and honored God and established a time of peace in the nation. Peace, however, did not last; it was shattered by an army from Egypt that invaded the territory of Judah. King Asa was prepared to defend his nation with an army of 300,000 men equipped with large shields and sharp spears and another 280,000 warriors equipped with small shields and bows and arrows. One problem remained, however: the army from Egypt was much larger than that of small Judah, having a million men. Besides having twice as many warriors, the Egyptians charged into the territory with three hundred chariots and horses, while Asa's army had none!

King Asa, however, wasn't worried; he was well aware of his limited forces, but he also knew he had something greater and more powerful than anything that could come from Egypt. He had the mighty God, the King of the Universe, on his side. Before confronting the enemy in battle, Asa prayed to God, "Lord, we are a powerless army against this mighty one. We are counting on you as we fight in your name. O Lord, help us now." God listened. With God's help and power King Asa and his warriors defeated the vast Egyptian army.

The Spirit of God came on Azariah son of Oded. (2 Chronicles 15:1)

While the king and his army were defending their people, God's Spirit was at work in a man named Azariah, the son of a prophet. The Spirit came upon Azariah and urged him to speak to the king. As King Asa and his army returned to the city of Jerusalem, celebrating what God had done for them, Azariah exited the city to go out and meet the warriors. He approached the victorious army as the troops came to a halt. Then Azariah, filled with God's Spirit, boldly and courageously addressed the king.

"King Asa, listen to me," Azariah said. "All you men of Judah listen to me too. The Lord is with you. He will stay near you if you stay near him. If you dedicate your lives to serving him, he will be with you. But if you forget about him, he will forget about you. Israel, the nation to our north, had trouble because its people forgot about God and worshipped heathen gods of wood and stone. Don't be like them. You must be strong in the Lord and follow him. Now go do what you have to do. Don't be discouraged, God will reward your actions."

Azariah went home, while King Asa continued to think about Azariah's pronouncement. Then the king made a plan to remind the people about God and worship him alone. He tore down the idols of wood and stone everywhere in the kingdom of Judah.

He rebuilt God's altar, which stood outside the Temple. Then he summoned the people of Judah to gather in Jerusalem. They made animal sacrifices to God and took an oath to serve the Lord with all their hearts. They shouted with joy, sang praises to God, and blew the trumpets and the rams' horns in celebration. And God surrounded his people with peace because they had returned to loving him because of the Spirit-inspired words of Azariah.

The Spirit Today

As a prophet, Azariah was in God's service to speak on behalf of God to the king and the people. But to deliver the exact message at the right time and motivate the king to seek a second victory—one of reform within the nation's religious life—Azariah required a boost of courage and boldness from the Spirit. Azariah's message—"God will be near us if we remain near to him"—is repeated with a slight variation by the New Testament writer: "Come near to God and he will come near to you" (James 4:8). These words, inspired by the Spirit, pertain to every time and every age. We need to continually examine ourselves to renew our closeness to God and live always in the power of the Spirit.

—

The Spirit Fills Jahaziel with Encouraging Words

from 2 Chronicles 20:1–28

When Jehoshaphat, a man who loved and honored God, became king of Judah, he attentively listened to God's prophets and obediently followed their instructions. On the day he heard the terrifying news that a combined army from Moab and Ammon was marching toward the city of Jerusalem, King Jehoshaphat desperately turned to God for help. Out in the courtyard of the Temple, King Jehoshaphat prayed, "Lord God of our ancestors, you rule all the kingdoms of the earth. You possess power and might, and no one can oppose you. We know you will hear us and save us. We don't know what to do, so we are looking to you for help."

Then the Spirit of the LORD came on Jahaziel son of Zechariah,...a Levite and descendant of Asaph, as he stood in the assembly. (2 Chronicles 20:14)

As Jahaziel, one of the workers in the Temple, listened to King Jehoshaphat's prayer, God's Spirit came upon him without a sound, urging him to step forward and supplying him with the right words to speak to the king. Boldly stepping out from the Temple into the courtyard, Jahaziel faced Jehoshaphat as well as the great crowd that had congregated there.

In a clear, loud voice, Jahaziel said, "Everyone pay attention to me. King Jehoshaphat, hear what I say, because the Lord has told me to tell you this. This battle that you are about to wage against the enemy isn't yours—it belongs to God. Tomorrow when you go into battle against the Moabites and Ammonites, don't be afraid of this massive army. Go out and face them bravely and confidently, because the Lord will be with you. Take your position on the battlefield and then stand still. You won't have to fight. Just wait and see how God supplies you with the victory."

King Jehoshaphat was overjoyed with this announcement, knowing that God had answered his prayer! He bowed down in the courtyard, lowering his face to the ground. Then all the people followed his example, bowing down in praise to God for this good news! With the promise of deliverance in their minds, the Temple musicians marched out into the crowd, singing songs of praise to God and celebrating the coming victory.

The next day, as King Jehoshaphat and his army readied themselves for battle, the king stood before his troops to reassure his warriors. "Listen to me," the king commanded. "Trust the Lord your God. Believe what Jahaziel said and you will succeed."

The king then did a very unusual thing: he assigned a choir from the Temple musicians to sing praises to God while leading the army out of the city and onto the battlefield. The choir sang and shouted as the army marched out to face the enemy troops: "Thank the Lord our God, for his mercy endures forever!"

What God's Spirit had foretold through Jahaziel happened later that day. The army of Judah arrived in the desert and did not have to fight, since God had already caused the enemy soldiers to turn on one another and fight among themselves. King Jehoshaphat led the troops back to Jerusalem, rejoicing that God had been victorious over their enemy.

The Spirit Today

"Stand still, watch and wait. God's got this." Long ago that message came to the Israelites through Moses on the shores of the Red Sea as God's people faced the fury of Pharaoh's army. In spite of their doubts and fearfulness, God worked a miracle. A similar message and result occurred in Jahaziel's time. Sometimes we yearn to hear a message as direct as those from the Spirit to reassure us. In fact, the Spirit does speak today, not in the words of a prophet or in a voice from out of the sky, but through an inner voice, when we come near to God. If you've ever been at the end of your rope, with absolutely no idea of what to do, perhaps you have recalled the slogan of a famous twelve-step program that states the same message this way: "Let go and let God." They are slightly different words but the same message that came to God's people "back in the day." If we stand still and listen, the Spirit will speak and reassure us that "God's got this." "Do not be anxious about anything, but in every situation, by prayer and petition, with thanksgiving, present your requests to God" (Phil. 4:6).

—

The Spirit Moves a Priest to Action

from 2 Chronicles 24:1–21

Although he was only seven years old, Joash became king of God's people. Because he ruled under the advice and guidance of a priest named Jehoiada, Joash was a good king who loved God and followed the Law of Moses. For many, many years the nation did not go to war. Peace reigned on all the borders of the nation of Judah.

Shortly after Jehoiada died, however, King Joash changed. Without his wise adviser to guide him, the king became lax in following God's laws and being obedient to him. Rather than surrounding himself with alternate wise advisers, Joash heeded the advice of some foolish people. While the priests faithfully continued their duties in the Temple, Joash turned away from the traditions, ceased serving God, and began worshipping man-made statues carved from wood and stone. Out of loyalty to their king, most of the people in Judah drifted away from God too, forgetting God's goodness and blessings, shunning his laws and commands, and adopting the cultural practices of those who worshipped the local gods. As a result God became angry with his people for ignoring him.

One day the priest Zechariah, the son of the great priest Jehoiada, was in the courtyard of the Temple performing his priestly duties at the altar, when God's Spirit came upon him, urging him to speak to the people about their evil behavior. As Zechariah walked into the crowded courtyard of the Temple, the Spirit filled him with boldness and provided him with the appropriate words. "Why are you breaking God's rules?" Zechariah asked the people. "Your lives won't be good if you keep disobeying God. The Lord will take away his blessings, and you won't live in peace. Listen to me and heed my warning: since you've turned your backs on God, he will turn his back on you."

Then the Spirit of God came on Zechariah son of Jehoiada the priest. (2 Chronicles 24:20)

The people were shocked and offended. They were furious that Zechariah would dare to reprimand them and tell them what to do. Almost immediately a group of angry men united together and devised a scheme to rid themselves of Zechariah and his out-spokenness. They even successfully secured the king's approval.

One day as Zechariah prepared an offering for God at the altar, the same group of angry men, equipped with huge stones, walked into the Temple courtyard. Without a word they took aim and hurled the rocks at Zechariah's head, making him bleed and knock-ing him to the ground. Mortally wounded, Zecha-riah called out to God, "Lord, I know you can see what is happening. Pay these men back for their evil actions." Then Zechariah the priest died in front of the holy Temple. God's Spirit had worked in him to speak for God to the people. Rather than saying what the people wanted to hear, he spoke the words that the Spirit had given him.

The Spirit Today

Zechariah experienced the Spirit's power as he spoke out boldly for God even as he faced hostile opposition. The Spirit moved this way many years later in the apostle Peter, who was filled with the Holy Spirit when he spoke to the rulers and elders in the church (Acts 4:8–22), not certain of what their response would be to his outspokenness. The Spirit still fills people today with boldness: "For the Spirit God gave us does not make us timid, but gives us power" (2 Tim. 1:7). If we live in the Spirit, we must always walk, act, and speak as followers of Jesus. Pray that the Spirit will enable you to be brave and speak boldly in the name of Christ and in Christian love whenever you can—even if the response and outcome are uncertain.

Chapter Four

The Spirit Inspires the Prophets

"For prophecy never had its origin in the human
will, but prophets, though human, spoke from
God as they were carried along by the Holy Spirit."

2 Peter 1:21

Over time God's people forgot how much God loved
them. They started to worship other gods and bow
down to idols of wood and stone, thinking the heathen gods, rather than the true living God, provided
the spring rain, the sunshine, the harvest, and their
well-being. The people didn't think anything would
happen, but when God's people snubbed him, God
got angry. He tried to wake up the people with powerful words about the consequences of disobeying his
law. Through the Spirit, God spoke to the prophets

of punishment and judgment, but the people didn't listen and the people didn't change.

Then one day the armies of the great Babylonian empire swept over the nations, including the nation of Israel. The warriors ripped apart the Temple. They grabbed the gold serving pieces and stashed them in their packs. They took the candlesticks and the gold plates. They stole the gold shields and cut up the embroidered curtains. They even took some of the people captive and deported them to other countries. Others were left behind in a devastated land of trampled fields, destroyed forests, and burned-out buildings. The walls of Jerusalem were left in heaps of stone and crumbled mortar.

God's people might have forgotten God, but he didn't forget them. He still loved them and had a plan for them. Even when things were not going well, when life was hard and evil seemed to be winning, God gave his people hope for the future. He called people who became known as prophets to speak for him, to stand up and say words that others wouldn't dare to speak. The words didn't come from the person; they came from the great Spirit of God. God's Spirit filled the prophets with insight and deep thoughts. Then he gave them the exact words to say to God's people, empowering the prophets' words and deeds.

Sometimes the people didn't listen. Sometimes

the people listened and got mad—really mad—at the prophet. Sometimes the people tried to hurt the person speaking for God, or to send him away, or to throw him in prison. But the prophets of God continued to speak the words God's Spirit told them to say.

The prophets also talked about the Spirit, sharing news of hope and a coming renewal as well as information about the nature of the Spirit.

The prophet Joel attributed these words to the Lord:

"And afterward,
I will pour out my Spirit on all people.
Your sons and daughters will prophesy,
your old men will dream dreams,
your young men will see visions.
Even on my servants, both men and women,
I will pour out my Spirit in those days."

(Joel 2:28)

The prophet Isaiah knew the Spirit provided him with the right words to say—he didn't have to do it on his own. He declared, "The Spirit of the Sovereign LORD is on me, because the LORD has anointed me to proclaim good news to the poor" (Isa. 61:1).

Isaiah's message was a special one to the people of the time in which he lived as well as to future generations. God chose him to prophesy about the coming Messiah, the One who would change everything, the One who would save the world:

> *The Spirit of the LORD will rest on him—*
> *the Spirit of wisdom and of understanding,*
> *the Spirit of counsel and of might,*
> *the Spirit of the knowledge and fear of the*
>   *LORD—*
> *and he will delight in the fear of the LORD.*
>   (Isaiah 11:2–3)

> *"Here is my servant, whom I uphold,*
> *my chosen one in whom I delight;*
> *I will put my Spirit on him,*
> *and he will bring justice to the nations."*
>   (Isaiah 42:1)

> *"As for me, this is my covenant with them," says*
>   *the LORD. "My Spirit, who is on you, will not*
>   *depart from you, and my words that I have put*
>   *in your mouth will always be on your lips, on*
>   *the lips of your children and on the lips of their*
>   *descendants—from this time on and forever,"*
> *says the LORD.*
>   (Isaiah 59:21)

The prophets were God's voice, bringing news of the future, justice, and judgment on the wicked nations, and also bringing hope for a later time when God's Spirit would live in all people. Four different times God clearly conveyed to Ezekiel to tell the people that the Spirit would come (Ezek. 11:19; 36:26–27; 37:14; 39:29). God made a promise: "I will put my Spirit in them. Then they will follow my decrees and keep my laws. They will be my people, and I will be their God."

The Spirit Encounters Ezekiel

from Ezekiel 1–3

Ezekiel lived in exile in Babylon years before the Babylonians annihilated Jerusalem and its people with a final ruthless invasion and destruction. Having already spent five years in captivity, Ezekiel had settled in the land near the Kebar River. He was destined to be a priest, but he now lived far

> The Spirit came into me and raised me to my feet, and I heard him speaking to me. (Ezekiel 2:2)

from the holy Temple of God in Jerusalem and would be deprived of his calling to present offerings to the Lord on the altar and serve in the sanctuary. During the year in which he turned thirty years old, however, while he was alone on the banks of the river, he was overwhelmed by the presence of the divine. God's hand was on him, and he saw visions of God's glory. When he saw a form similar to a man but also like a radiant rainbow, Ezekiel fell down, touching his face to the ground. Then the voice of God said, "Stand up, Ezekiel. I have something important to say to you."

As God spoke, the Spirit pervaded Ezekiel's being and stood him up on his feet. Then God continued. "Go to the Israelites, my people, even though they have rebelled against me. Tell them exactly what I have to say, whether they listen to you or not. Don't be afraid of them. Do not fear what they do or what they say to you or even what they say about you. Always keep talking. Repeat my exact words, introducing your message every time with these words: 'This is what the Lord says.'"

As God finished giving his instructions, the Spirit grabbed hold of Ezekiel, lifted him up, and whisked him away. Suddenly Ezekiel realized that the Spirit had deposited him among the community of exiles in Tel Aviv near the river. Ezekiel, bitter, distressed, and furious because he had to inform God's people of their imminent punishment and doom, sat down in silence for seven days. When the week was over, God spoke to Ezekiel again and instructed him: "You are obligated to speak out to the people and point out their wickedness. I will hold you responsible for this task. Now get up and go out to the plain, and I'll speak to you there."

Ezekiel did as God commanded. When he arrived on the plain, the glory of the Lord filled the area. The exact same glory that Ezekiel had first witnessed at the river appeared a second time, causing him to fall down in awe and reverence. Then the Spirit overpowered Ezekiel, took hold of him, stood him up on his feet, and told him, "Go back home, Ezekiel, and stay in your house. You'll be unable to leave the house or mingle with the people in town. I'll make your tongue stick to the roof of your mouth so you can't preach. You won't be able to point out the people's sinful ways to them or encourage them to change. You won't be able to utter a word until I speak to you; then I'll open your mouth and give you the words to say. But every speech you give must begin with, 'This is what the Sovereign Lord says.' Some people will listen to you, others will not."

The Spirit Today

The stories in Ezekiel are vivid and captivating; they pique our imaginations and create memorable pictures. While reading Ezekiel, we can clearly recognize the words supplied by the Spirit to the prophet through the statement "This is what the Sovereign Lord says" before a declaration.

Today the Spirit moves people to ministry or teaching God's Word, the Bible. His provision of words may not always be as direct as it was to the prophets, but he inspires people to preach, working through their minds, abilities, wisdom, and knowledge of the word of the Lord.

In many worship services, after the liturgist reads from the Bible, he or she states, "This is the word of the Lord" as a prophet might. The next time you hear God's Word read in church, whether or not that phrase is provided, remind yourself that the Bible is indeed the word of the Lord, inspired by the Spirit, and that the pastor presenting the message is in God's service through the work of the Spirit.

The Spirit Transports Ezekiel to Jerusalem

from Ezekiel 8–11, 43

> The Spirit lifted me up between earth and heaven and in visions of God he took me to Jerusalem, to the entrance of the north gate of the inner court, where the idol that provokes to jealousy stood. (Ezekiel 8:3)

About a year after God called Ezekiel to be his prophet, God appeared again to Ezekiel and presented the vision of a radiant man that Ezekiel had seen twice before. Then the Spirit grabbed hold of Ezekiel, lifted him up, moved him somewhere between heaven and earth, and finally deposited him hundreds of miles away in Jerusalem. Standing at the north gate of the courtyard of the Temple, Ezekiel saw for himself the sinful practices that had forced God to judge the people of Israel: idol worship and pagan rituals, wall illustrations of unclean animals and crawling creatures, and injustice and violent slaughter. While Ezekiel stood and watched, the Lord spoke to him, and spectacular images appeared: cherubim with wings and four faces, wheels spinning within wheels, and magnificent living creatures. Then the glory of the Lord, which had inhabited the Temple for centuries, rose from the Temple and exited the building along with the wheels and the creatures.

Once again the Spirit lifted Ezekiel up and physically moved him from the north gate of the Temple courtyard to the gate on the east side. The Spirit filled Ezekiel with a prophecy to give the leaders of Israel. "This is what the Sovereign Lord says: 'You've killed hundreds of people in Jerusalem. Now I will bring the sword of the enemy against you. I'll drive you out of the city and allow you to be punished by your enemies. You have ignored my decrees and broken my laws and replaced them with the pagan standards of neighboring nations.' "

After hearing these words of judgment, Ezekiel, terribly distressed, fell down and shouted, "Oh no, God! Are you going to destroy everyone in Israel? Will there be no one left?"

"Share this message with my people, Ezekiel," God answered. " 'Although I sent them away from their land and scattered them among the nations, I will gather them together again and bring them home to their land. I will unite their hearts and put a new Spirit in them. Then they will follow my decrees and obey my laws. They will be my people and I will be their God.' "

Once again the glory of the Lord rose from within Jerusalem and departed, moving toward the mountain in the east. Then the Spirit lifted Ezekiel up and carried him back to the exiles in Babylon. As soon as the vision provided by the Spirit left, Ezekiel recognized his surroundings and proceeded to retell all that had happened to him.

When the Babylonians finally destroyed the city of Jerusalem, they took more people captive and reduced God's holy Temple to a heap of smoldering ruins. In their land of exile, the Israelites grieved over the loss of the Temple—their nation's pride and glory. The image of a destroyed city and violated Temple shattered their future dreams of going home and returning to their former lives

> Then the Spirit lifted me up and brought me into the inner court, and the glory of the LORD filled the temple. (Ezekiel 43:5)

and ways of worship, but God had a plan. Through the Spirit, Ezekiel was about to witness the Temple's restoration.

On April 28, 573 BC, during the beginning of the Jewish New Year and twenty-five years into the exile, the presence of God's Spirit overpowered Ezekiel again. The powerful hand of the Lord seized Ezekiel, and through visions Ezekiel saw a city in the land of

Israel. A mysterious man who appeared in bronze escorted Ezekiel on a tour of the area. Ezekiel saw the city walls, the massive iron gates, and the courtyards of the Temple. Realizing this was the city of Jerusalem, Ezekiel ventured toward the Temple building, which was standing as before, complete with its porticos, its two outer and inner sanctuaries, and the Most Holy Place. The bronze-like man measured every wall and room as they explored the building. When he had completed all the measurements, the man escorted Ezekiel to the east gate of Jerusalem.

Looking toward the east, Ezekiel witnessed something rising like the sun. He heard God's voice roar like the water in a rushing river and saw the land all around him glow with light. This spectacular sight was the appearance of the glory of God! Then a vision of God flashed in front of him. At the sight Ezekiel knelt down and lowered his face to the ground in awe and reverence. Then the power of the Spirit lifted Ezekiel up and transported him directly to the inner court of the Temple. As he stood inside the Temple court, Ezekiel witnessed God's glory move from the east into the Temple area. The glory of the Lord settled on the building, filling the holy Temple, just as it had in the time of Solomon. Then Ezekiel heard a voice from inside the Temple say, "This Temple is the place of my throne and my footstool. This is where I will live with the Israelites forever. Write down the design and the exact measurements of my house, Ezekiel. Describe every detail to the people so they will faithfully rebuild my holy dwelling. After Jerusalem is restored, its name will be 'The Lord is there.' For here is where I will live with my people forever."

The Spirit Today

Ezekiel's experiences with the Spirit broaden our perceptions and understanding of the Spirit's power and ability. Only two people, Ezekiel (Ezek. 8:3; 43:5) and Philip (Acts 8:39) experienced the Spirit's ability to physically transport an individual. Our understanding of this "teleporting" makes us think of an episode of *Star Trek*—it's exotic and mysterious, and we're uncertain how it occurs. There are some things God has not revealed to us; the Spirit's ability to lift up and physically transport a person is one of these mysteries of God. Perhaps someday we will come to understand it, but until we do, we should allow for the possibility of things yet unknown and not be frightened by the unexplainable. We don't need to know the physics behind it, we need to be in awe of the Spirit's capacity to accomplish it and be reassured that if he is capable of doing something outside our realm of understanding, he is most qualified to handle what we know he has done and continues to do for us.

—

The Spirit Revives Dry Bones

from Ezekiel 37

God's Spirit again came to Ezekiel while he was an exile in Babylon. He scooped up Ezekiel, carried him away in the air, and placed him down in a mysterious land—a large, open valley full of dried-out bones bleached white by the sun.

> The hand of the LORD was on me, and he brought me out by the Spirit of the LORD and set me in the middle of the valley; it was full of bones. (Ezekiel 37:1)

The Spirit turned to Ezekiel and said, "What do you think, Ezekiel, do you think these dead bones can come alive again?"

"I'm not sure," Ezekiel answered. "The bones are dry and scattered all over the place. Only you know the answer to that question."

"Call out to the bones, Ezekiel," the Spirit said. "Speak to them these words from the Lord: 'Look, bones, I'm going to put you together again. I'll put muscle on you and cover you with skin. And then I'll breathe into you and make you alive again.'"

Ezekiel did as the Spirit had instructed. He shouted to the bones in the valley the promising words of the Lord. Suddenly Ezekiel heard rattling coming from the valley; the bones rose from the ground and started to dance. They jostled into position; leg bones joined pelvic bones, arm bones attached to shoulders, skulls moved into position on the spine. Piece by piece the bones merged into human skeletons. As the skeletons danced, muscle and flesh formed over the bones, then skin appeared and covered the human forms.

The Spirit of God instructed Ezekiel to summon the wind to breathe air into the bodies. So Ezekiel called out, "Come, Spirit-Wind, from east and west, from north and south. Breathe your breath into these bodies and make them alive again." The wind obeyed, and the Spirit breathed the breath of life into the bodies, just as he had on the sixth day of creation

when Adam was created. The bodies inhaled the
Spirit-Wind and came alive. They stood up on their
feet and assembled, resembling a great army ready for
action.

Then the Spirit explained to Ezekiel, "These bones
represent the people of God, who were once old and
broken and without hope. They were dead, but they
will come alive again someday. Now go back to the
people with this exact message from God: 'I judged
you, my people, because of your actions. You forgot
about my holy name and worshipped idols of wood
and stone. You hated my laws and disobeyed my
commandments. So I forced you out of your homes
and scattered you across the nations. But in time I
will forgive your sins. I will take away your hearts of
stone and give you new hearts. I will put my Spirit
in you and write my commandments on your hearts
so you can follow them. You will return to the land
I gave to your ancestors long ago. I will resettle your
towns and rebuild your ruins. The grain will grow
again in the fields, and the fruit trees will be loaded
with fruit. I will renew your spirits and renew your
land. I will be your God and you will be my people.'"

Suddenly Ezekiel was back with the exiled people.
He recounted his experience with the Spirit and the
dry bones in the valley, carefully repeating what God

had told him to say. The people listened to Ezekiel and believed what he shared with them. Once again God's people, although far from their homeland, were filled with joy and hope for a future of renewal and restoration. Once again they trusted God to bring them home again.

The Spirit Today

Ezekiel's vision of the dry bones was highly symbolic to the exiles of the time, who felt broken and dead, forgotten by God. The resurrection scene showed the exiles that God would remember them and revive them to a new beginning.

Although our circumstances are different from those of the ancient Jews in exile, the story speaks of the Spirit's work in the world today and shows us what God is promising. The Spirit is at work in broken lives and spirits. He renews and restores and gives new life. Just as he was capable of bringing bones back from the dead and total decay, restoring them with breath of life and a new Spirit, he is able to renew believers today. "Be filled with the Spirit" (Eph. 5:18).

The Spirit Reveals a Mystery to Daniel

from Daniel 1–2, 5

Daniel and his three friends were Jewish teenagers when they were taken captive in Jerusalem and forced to move to Babylon. Because they were young and smart and from the royal families of Israel, the four young men were chosen to serve in the court of the king of Babylon. Although these captives were far from their familiar surroundings, God was with them through his Spirit, providing them with knowledge and wisdom to deal with the challenges of life in the royal Babylonian court. Daniel also had a special gift, much like Joseph; he could explain people's dreams and tell their meaning.

> To these four young men God gave knowledge and understanding of all kinds of literature and learning. And Daniel could understand visions and dreams of all kinds. (Daniel 1:17)

One night the king of Babylon, named Nebuchadnezzar, had a spectacular dream that forced him awake. Upset and unable to get back to sleep, he yelled out to his servants, "Summon all the wise men in my kingdom. Tell them to come to the palace immediately!"

In the middle of the night, the magicians, enchanters, sorcerers, and astrologers from all over the kingdom hurried to the king. When everyone was present in Nebuchadnezzar's bedchamber, he said to them, "I had a dream tonight that really bothers me. Now I'm upset and I can't sleep. I have to know what it means. Someone must tell me what the dream is and what it means. If you don't, I will kill you and turn your houses into piles of rubbish. But if you do tell me the dream and its meaning, I'll shower you with money and make you famous in the kingdom."

"Oh, Your Majesty," said one of the sorcerers, "we certainly are able to tell you what your dream means, but first you have to disclose the dream to us."

"Absolutely not!" shouted the king. "You're stalling for more time. *You* must tell me what I dreamed and also tell me the meaning."

"But no one on earth can do that," replied an astrologer. "And no king, not even the most powerful and great in all the world, has ever made such a request as you have. Your demand is impossible. Only the gods could do something like this, and they don't live here with us."

The king was furious and barked out an order, "Arioch, you are the commander of my guards.

Round up all the wise men in my kingdom, including the new captives from Judah, and kill them all."

Arioch went looking for the captives from Judah: Daniel, Hananiah, Mishael, and Azariah. Daniel, being very wise and capable of handling any situation, asked Arioch what was going on. When he heard the story, Daniel hurried to the palace, requested to see the king, and asked for additional time to fulfill the king's request. Surprisingly, the king said yes.

> During the night the mystery was revealed to Daniel in a vision. (Daniel 2:19)

Daniel, Hananiah, Mishael, and Azariah prayed to God, asking him to tell them the secret of the king's dream—what it was and what it meant—so that the lives of all the wise men in Babylon would be spared. When the young men finished praying, they headed to bed. During the night, God's Spirit sent Daniel a vision, revealing to him the king's secret.

The next day Daniel hurried to the palace to present the findings to King Nebuchadnezzar. "No wise man, enchanter, magician, or fortune-teller can tell you your secret," Daniel said, "but there is a God in heaven whom I serve who reveals such secrets. Last night he gave me a vision about your dream and what it means. My God has shown you what is going to happen in the future.

"In your dream you saw a shiny giant statue of a man that frightened you. His head was made of gold. His chest and arms were made of silver. His stomach and thighs were bronze. His legs were iron. And his feet were clay mixed with iron. All of a sudden a gigantic rock broke away from the mountain, rolled into the statue, and smashed it into tiny pieces. Then the wind blew everything away.

"Now here's what it all means. The God of heaven has given you power, strength, and honor; you are the head of gold. When your kingdom comes to an end, another kingdom, the silver part, will rule. When that kingdom falls, a third kingdom of bronze will rule the earth, then one of iron. The last one will be divided into a strong part of iron, and a weak part of clay. The rock is God's kingdom that will come and crush all the other kingdoms of the world. Then God will rule the earth."

King Nebuchadnezzar said to Daniel, "Your God is the greatest of all gods. He is the Lord over kings. He reveals mysteries and tells you the secrets of the world."

Then the king made Daniel ruler over the province of Babylon, and the leader of all the wise men in the nation.

Many years later, Daniel served another king in Babylon by the name of Belshazzar. One night King Belshazzar threw a huge party, inviting a thousand people to join him for a feast. Since he wanted to make the party special, he told his servants, "Bring out the gold and silver wine cups that King Nebuchadnezzar took from the Temple in Jerusalem. I want my guests to see their beauty and drink fine wine out of them."

The servants followed the order, brought out the special golden wine cups, and placed them on the banquet tables. At dinner, the king and his guests drank wine from the gold cups and toasted their gods using the sacred cups from God's Temple. While they raised the cups high in the air, a hand and fingers suddenly appeared in the air by the wall in the back of the room. One of the fingers scrolled out these words: *Mene, Mene, Tekel,* and *Parsin.* Then the hand vanished.

As King Belshazzar watched the hand in motion, his face turned pale. His knees knocked together, and his legs got weak. He was so scared he fell to the floor. Then he shouted, "Call the enchanters, the astrologers, and the fortune-tellers. Gather all the wise men from my kingdom. Whoever can read this writing and tell me what it means will be honored with gold jewelry and purple robes and rule part of my kingdom!"

As soon as possible all the wise men, astrologers, fortune-tellers, and enchanters of Babylon gathered in the dining room. They looked at the words on the wall; they looked at one another and shook their heads. They had no idea what the words written on the wall meant. Seeing their bewilderment, the king became more scared than he had been.

> There is a man in your kingdom who has the spirit of the holy gods in him. In the time of your father he was found to have insight and intelligence and wisdom like that of the gods. (Daniel 5:11)

As soon as the queen mother heard what was going on, she went to the banquet hall and said to the king, "Don't be so scared. Don't look so pale. There's a man in your kingdom who is special. He can handle this. During Nebuchadnezzar's time he was wise and had divine knowledge. He can interpret dreams, explain riddles, and solve difficult problems. I'm sure he can handle this. His name is Daniel, and he will tell you what the writing means. Someone should go find him."

When Daniel arrived at the banquet hall, he noticed the enchanters, fortune-tellers, and astrologers were quiet and embarrassed. As Daniel scanned the words on the wall, King Belshazzar asked him, "Are you Daniel, one of the captives from Judah? I've heard that you are wise, that you can interpret dreams and solve difficult problems, and that the spirit of the holy gods lives in you. None of my wise men can tell me the meaning of the words. If you can do it, I'll give you gold jewelry and purple robes and let you rule part of my kingdom."

Daniel calmly turned to the king and said, "Keep your gifts and give them to someone else. But I'll tell you what the words mean. The Most High God rules over the kingdoms of the world and appoints anyone he desires to rule over them. He has appointed you, and yet you have not honored him. You have not humbled yourself before him. In fact you have defied him by drinking wine from the sacred cups from his Temple in Jerusalem and praising gods made of wood and stone. You have not honored the God who gives you the breath of life and controls your future. So he has written this message. And this is what it means. God has numbered your days as king and they will end soon. You have been weighed on the balance of justice and have not measured up. Your kingdom has been divided and given to the Medes and the Persians."

The king had rightfully been anxious about the message on the wall. That same night, the Medes and the Persians invaded the city. They killed King Belshazzar, and a new king, Darius, king of the Medes, took over his kingdom.

The Spirit Today

God gifted individuals like Daniel to protect his people wherever they lived and to testify to unbelievers around them that the Spirit of God, the Spirit of light and life, not the power of darkness, was working in them. Daniel's wisdom and knowledge brought King Nebuchadnezzar to the realization that Daniel's God was indeed the greatest of all gods (Dan. 2:47).

Even today the Spirit comes into our lives, giving us gifts so we can help one another, build up the body of Christ (the church), and be witnesses to unbelievers (Rom. 12:4–8). Just as Daniel's wisdom was from God, our wisdom also comes from the Spirit if we live in the Spirit: "This is what we speak, not in words taught us by human wisdom but in words taught by the Spirit, explaining spiritual realities with Spirit-taught words" (1 Cor. 2:13).

—

The Spirit Motivates the Refugees

from Ezra 1, 3–4, 6; Haggai 2:1–9; Zechariah 4:6

After many years, King Cyrus took over the rule of Babylon and the entire Persian Empire. As God had promised his people, the time had come for restoration and renewal. The Spirit worked in Cyrus's heart and moved him to make a significant announcement: "The God of heaven has made me ruler of this huge kingdom. He has told me to build a temple in Jerusalem for him. Any of God's people may now return to Jerusalem in Judah and begin rebuilding the Temple. May God be with you."

Although the people of Israel had settled down in Babylon and had established homes and families there, the Spirit worked in their hearts, inciting in them the desire to return to Jerusalem. They had lived in Babylon for seventy years, and many of them had never experienced life in their hometowns in Judah or seen the city of Jerusalem. Many had been children when they were captured and carried off; others had been born in captivity. They could recall only the stories told to them about this wonderful city and the land that God had given his people so long ago. But now they had the opportunity to be free—to return to the place they now yearned for, to rebuild what had been lost.

God's people were going home—just as he had promised them through his prophets. With the permission of the king, the people packed up their houses, gathered their children, and readied themselves to travel to Jerusalem. Their neighbors gave them silver and gold, horses, mules, camels and donkeys, money and supplies for their journey. King Cyrus returned all the beautiful utensils that had been stolen from God's Temple. He handed over the gold and silver dishes, cups and bowls, knives and forks, pitchers and platters. The preparations for the trip being complete, fifty thousand people left Babylon and began the journey back to Judah and the city of Jerusalem.

After months of travel and sufficient time to settle

in their former homes, the people gathered in the old city of Jerusalem and eagerly began rebuilding the Temple. They put in stones for the foundation in the place where the old Temple had stood. When they completed the foundation, some people cried and other people celebrated, thanking God and singing songs of praise. Their joyful voices rang out across the countryside, arousing the curiosity of the people living in the surrounding areas. The neighboring people hurried to Jerusalem to find out the reason for all the commotion. Realizing the Temple was being reconstructed, they offered their assistance. "We would really like to help you rebuild the Temple," they said to the leader, Zerubbabel.

"King Cyrus specifically commanded *us* to build this temple," Zerubbabel informed them. "We're building this temple for *our* God. We don't need your help."

The neighbors were furious that their offer had been rejected. In retaliation they harassed the people while they tried to work. They bullied them and stole their supplies. They even threatened to start a war. And after a while God's people got discouraged. They became so afraid of their neighbors that they put away their tools, packed up their supplies, and stopped building the Temple. The Temple was only about half-finished, and it remained that way for years, completely forgotten.

> "This is what I covenanted with you when you came out of Egypt. And my Spirit remains among you. Do not fear." (Haggai 2:5)

Twenty years passed, and no one bothered to work on the Temple. Then God spoke to the prophet Haggai and said, "Talk to Zerubbabel and the people who returned from Babylon. Tell them my house remains unfinished while they live in nice houses. Tell them not to be afraid, because my Spirit is with them. Then tell them to get back to work on building the Temple."

> So [the angel] said to me, "This is the word of the LORD to Zerubbabel: 'Not by might nor by power, but by my Spirit,' says the LORD Almighty." (Zechariah 4:6)

God also spoke to the prophet Zechariah: "Tell the people and their leaders that the Temple work will not get done through human strength. The completion of the Temple will only get done by the power of my Spirit. Nothing can stop him."

God's words, spoken by Haggai and Zechariah, as well as a letter from King Darius, inspired the returned exiles to pick up their tools and finish building God's Temple. With the reassurance that God's Spirit was with them and through the power of the Spirit, the workmen completed God's beautiful Temple in a few years. Then all the people gathered again in Jerusalem. The priests, the Temple workers, and all God's people celebrated for seven days the completion of God's holy Temple.

The Spirit Today

The people were so frightened, so battered and bullied, that they withdrew and concentrated on looking out for themselves and building their own insular lives. They didn't want any problems; they wanted to live in peace. But in that isolation they forgot about God and what was required of them—to build the Temple. Only through the Spirit-inspired words of the prophets and the assurance that the work would be done through God's power alone (Zech. 4:6) were they able to get back on track.

When difficulties occur in life, we often want to withdraw, to "live in peace," thinking that if we live in isolation, all will be well. But God calls believers to shine light in darkness (Matt. 5:14), to be a blessing to others, and to build up his church. He does not want us to live in fear, for he has provided the Spirit of power to be with us: "For the Spirit God gave us does not make us timid, but gives us power, love and self-discipline" (2 Tim. 1:7).

PART TWO

The Spirit's Work in the New Testament

During the four hundred years between the time the Jews returned to Jerusalem and the beginning of the history recorded in the New Testament, God's people waited for the promised Messiah and the "new Spirit" that the prophets had foretold. When the time was right, the Spirit interacted with God's chosen ones. The Spirit's interactions with people would be similar to the interactions he had had with God's people in the Old Testament, but not the same. He would continue to inspire people to great things, he would still make humble men into great leaders, but now he would do more. He would create human life in a virgin, commission God's Son to ministry, and come as the Comforter promised by Jesus. The dramatic event at Pentecost at last fulfilled the prophets' message of a new Spirit dwelling among God's people. The Spirit filled the disciples with power to preach the Good News of Jesus throughout the world, and promoted and sustained the growth of the church. That same Spirit continues to be with believers today, inspiring, sustaining, and comforting God's people throughout the world.

Chapter Five

The Spirit Works on God's Behalf

"The Spirit operates in nature and in the history of redemption to carry out the decrees and works of the Godhead."

Wick Broomall

The Spirit that witnessed creation and empowered God's people was about to participate in an act that is still difficult for the human mind to comprehend. He would combine the divine with humanity. Once again by working through an ordinary person— a young virgin woman—the Spirit would do the extraordinary: create new life in the form of a human but with the spirit of the divine. The Spirit executed God's plan to bring his Son to be born on earth and live among humans. He also revealed to certain people God's secrets, which mystified the majority, and called people to ministry.

Through the Spirit, God's plans and purposes for his people became a reality.

—

The Spirit Creates New Life in Mary

from Luke 1:26–39

Nazareth was an ordinary village, located in the farming region of Galilee, where the people lived simply. They cultivated trees that grew pomegranates, dates, grapes, and olives. They pressed the olives to make oil and squashed the grapes to make wine. They worshipped God in the local synagogue, following the Jewish laws and customs, and once a year they traveled to Jerusalem to celebrate the feast of the Passover. Other people considered anyone from Nazareth insignificant. God, however, was about to change that status, so that the name Nazareth would be known throughout the world for thousands of years. God chose a young girl named Mary from Nazareth to participate in his extraordinary plan. Mary was planning on becoming the wife of a local carpenter named Joseph. Her family had arranged the marriage but had yet to select a date for the ceremony. Mary and Joseph expected to lead an ordinary life after the wedding: they would live near their families; Joseph would work in his carpentry shop, and Mary would care for their home and any children God blessed them with. But God had a different plan for these two ordinary people from a less-than-ordinary town. God's Spirit would powerfully and mysteriously change everything from ordinary to extraordinary.

The angel answered, "The Holy Spirit will come on you, and the power of the Most High will overshadow you. So the holy one to be born will be called the Son of God." (Luke 1:35)

One day God sent the angel Gabriel to visit Mary and give her some surprising news.

"God has chosen you, Mary, to be the mother of his Son," the angel announced.

"How can that be possible?" Mary asked. "I've never been with a man. And I'm only engaged to Joseph."

"Your marital status doesn't matter to God. You'll become pregnant by the power of God's Spirit,"

Gabriel explained. "Your child will be the Son of God, and you will be his mother. Your relative Elizabeth is also expecting. By human standards she's entirely too old to be a mother, but she's already six months pregnant. You're not married and she's too old, but nothing is impossible for God to accomplish."

Mary was speechless, but she believed Gabriel and knew that this would actually happen. Mary humbly responded, "I am God's servant. I will do anything he asks me to do."

That night, while Mary was alone, God's Spirit came upon her. The Spirit of God, the Lord and Giver of Life, filled Mary; in an event unlike anything that had ever happened before in all time and in all places, Mary became pregnant with a child by God's Spirit.

Just as the Spirit of Life provided breath for Adam, the Spirit created a new life, a special life inside Mary's womb. This baby, created by the Holy Spirit, would be the divine Son of God and the human son of all people.

Mary awoke the next morning unaware that a miracle had occurred in the night. She remembered the angel Gabriel and the fascinating news he had brought her. Immediately she prepared for a visit to

Elizabeth and started on her journey to the hill country of Judea.

The Spirit Today

The virgin birth is a great mystery of the Christian faith, but a critical element in believing that Jesus was both human and divine. The power of the Spirit that came upon Mary and created the Son of God is the same Spirit who comes to us as unbelievers, gives us faith, and transforms us into new creatures in Christ. His activity in the universe is ongoing. He has great power (Rom. 15:19), capable of giving freedom and transforming the lives of people today (2 Cor. 3:17–18). He makes us realize God's love (Rom. 5:5) and gives us joy (1 Thess. 1:6).

His new life may not come as a child in the womb of a woman; he also brings new life into the hearts of people, turning the skeptic into a believer, doubt into certainty, despair into hope, and restoring wholeness to the broken. He comes upon people not to revert them to infancy but to transform the life already existing.

The Spirit Brings Great Joy

from Luke 1:39–79

On her three-day journey south to Judea, Mary thought about what the angel Gabriel had said. Would she really become pregnant? She wasn't married to Joseph yet. What would everyone in town say? And what would Joseph say? Who would believe that an angel had visited her? In the daylight the angel's visit sounded like an overly creative story. Was it all her imagination?

Mary calmed herself. Perhaps Elizabeth could give her advice. Maybe Zechariah, the priest, could help her understand...if *they* believed her. But first she needed to discover for herself if what the angel had told her was true—that Elizabeth was really pregnant.

At the door Mary called out, "Elizabeth, are you here? It's me, Mary."

> When Elizabeth heard Mary's greeting, the baby leaped in her womb, and Elizabeth was filled with the Holy Spirit. (Luke 1:41)

As soon as Elizabeth heard Mary's voice, Elizabeth felt her baby move. God's Spirit, the Spirit of Joy, caused the baby to leap for joy in his mother's womb.

The women looked at each other knowing they shared a bond. God had accomplished the impossible for both of them: one was married but too old to have a baby; the other was young enough, but not in the proper relationship to conceive a child. In the moment they embraced, the Spirit settled on Elizabeth and filled her with words of praise.

"You're radiant, Mary!" Elizabeth exclaimed. "You're going to be a mother—a special mother of a special baby! I'm so honored that you've come—that I'm privileged to speak to the mother of my Lord and King! You are blessed."

Mary shared with Elizabeth her story about Gabriel's visit. She recalled word for word what he had said. After talking to Elizabeth, Mary was positive that Gabriel's visit had indeed occurred, it wasn't a dream or something she'd imagined. She believed everything Gabriel had announced would come true.

Then Elizabeth shared the story of Gabriel's visit to Zechariah in the Temple. She explained to Mary how the angel had arrived and announced that she and Zechariah would have a child after all the years of being childless. The angel also announced that the child would be a special prophet named John, who would be filled with the Holy Spirit to declare the coming of the Messiah.

Gabriel had made two visits to announce a birth. Mary and Elizabeth would bring children into the world who would be exceptional—John, Elizabeth's son, would be filled with the Holy Spirit and would announce the coming of the Messiah. Mary's son, Jesus, would be the Son of God, the long-awaited Savior of Israel, the King of the Jews. For the next several months, Mary and Elizabeth shared their thoughts and concerns. After a three-month visit, Mary returned to her home in the little village of Nazareth.

When Elizabeth and Zechariah's son was born, their neighbors and relatives were ecstatic. They were excited and surprised that such old, old people could possibly have a healthy baby. As was the custom in those days, family and friends gathered at the house when the baby was eight days old to hear what the boy's name would be. They waited for Zechariah to announce the name of his son, assuming he would be named after his father. But Elizabeth spoke up instead. "No, his name isn't Zechariah!" she exclaimed. "His name is John." (She knew this because the angel had told them to name him that.)

But all the folks there were puzzled. "But that can't be," they said. "There's no one in your family named

John. The baby must be named after someone in the family. It's always been done that way." They gestured to Zechariah, who was unable to speak. He had been voiceless for the last nine months because he hadn't believed Gabriel's news. Zechariah motioned for someone to get him something to write on. He took the piece of wood and wrote, "His name is John." And at that moment Zechariah suddenly was able to speak. The people were shocked—not only about the baby's name but also because Zechariah could talk again!

His father Zechariah was filled with the Holy Spirit and prophesied. (Luke 1:67)

The Holy Spirit rested on Zechariah and filled him with joy, supplying him with the words to a marvelous song. As he held his son in his arms, Zechariah sang:

"Praise be to the Lord, the God of Israel,
because he has come to his people and redeemed
them.
And you, my child, will be called a prophet of the
Most High;
for you will go on before the Lord to prepare the
way for him,

> *to give his people the knowledge of salvation*
> *through the forgiveness of their sins,*
> *because of the tender mercy of our God,*
> *by which the rising sun will come to us from*
>   *heaven*
> *to shine on those living in darkness*
> *and in the shadow of death,*
> *to guide our feet into the path of peace."*

Throughout the hill country of Judea everyone was talking about this boy named John, his elderly mother, and his father, who suddenly was able to speak again.

"It is all so strange," they said, shaking their heads. "A baby born to old folks, a father who couldn't talk for nine months and then suddenly could, and a mother who insisted on giving him a strange name. What do you think this child will be? For sure God has something special planned for him."

The Spirit Today

Usually great joy accompanies the news of the birth of a baby. Social media lights up with pictures and words of congratulation from parents and grandparents announcing the news. The news of John's birth was a surprising miracle to the villagers who had known Zechariah and Elizabeth as the aging couple who remained childless. Their joy was extra special; it was not only for the birth of a healthy child but also for the miracle of birth at their advanced ages. Zechariah experienced a Spirit-infused joy that caused him to burst into a song of praise and thanks to God. This kind of great joy is available to us today through the Spirit. The Spirit promises joy as one of the gifts or rewards for believing and walking with the Spirit of God. "The fruit of the Spirit is love, joy, peace, forbearance, kindness, goodness, faithfulness, gentleness and self-control" (Gal. 5:22–23). Live in the joy of the Spirit, and let your life show it.

—

The Spirit Reveals a Promise

from Luke 2:25–35

Simeon, a devoted Jew, loved God, followed the Jewish laws, and walked to the Temple in Jerusalem to worship God regularly. The Holy Spirit had rested on Simeon, remaining with him, eventually helping him realize that he would live long enough to see the Promised One, the Messiah. This was an exciting revelation for Simeon, and he was confident it would happen even though he did not know when or where such an event would occur.

One day the Spirit inspired Simeon to walk to the Temple and see what was happening in the courtyard. Simeon didn't know whom he might see or what he would witness, he just knew he should be present in the Temple area. Now a few weeks earlier, in the little town of Bethlehem, a woman named Mary and her husband Joseph had welcomed their baby boy into the world. On the same day that Simeon decided to go to the Temple, they too were on their way, to present their child to God.

Simeon set out from his house and walked through the streets of Jerusalem toward the Temple Mount. He climbed the thirty-one steps to the Temple area, stopping on each landing to catch his breath. When he reached the entrance, the gatekeepers opened the golden gates for him, and Simeon entered a spacious courtyard. People were milling about. Everyone was busy talking and presenting special offerings to God. Simeon surveyed the people as he entered the courtyard outside the Temple. Then he saw them—a young woman carrying an infant, guided tenderly by a man who was carrying a cage containing two doves. There was something special about the couple that made them stand out for Simeon.

As Simeon moved closer to get a better look at the little family, they suddenly disappeared from his view. When he saw them again, they were coming out of the Nicanor Gate in the Court of Women, where the priests dedicated children to God. As Simeon came up to them, he looked closely at the baby. "Who are you?" Simeon asked the girl.

"I'm Mary, and this is Joseph," Mary explained. "We're from the town of Nazareth, and have come to Jerusalem to present an offering to God because I recently had a baby. His name is Jesus. And since he's our firstborn child, we came to dedicate him to God."

It had been revealed to him [Simeon] by the Holy Spirit that he would not die before he had seen the Lord's Messiah. (Luke 2:26)

Then Mary handed the infant Jesus to the old man. As Simeon cradled the baby in his arms, God's Spirit opened Simeon's eyes. Suddenly he realized he was looking at the face of the Messiah, the Savior that all Israel had been waiting for! Simeon's face lit up, and God's Spirit filled him with joy. Looking up to heaven, he praised God and prayed: "Oh Lord God, as you have promised, I can now leave this life in peace because I've seen the One who is the Savior. He is the light that will bring hope and salvation to all the nations. He will bring glory to your people, Israel."

Mary and Joseph looked at each other, amazed at what the old man had said about their baby boy. Handing the baby back to Mary, Simeon gave them this blessing: "Go in peace. May the Lord be with you." Then the Spirit within Simeon made him prophesy, "Your son is special. In his lifetime he will cause many people to be lost and others to be saved. The thoughts of those who reject him will come to light. And your heart will break with sorrow."

The Spirit Today

The Spirit had lived in Simeon for a long time; as a result of that closeness, the Spirit had revealed a secret to him—that before he died he would see the long-promised Messiah. As believers we are promised the presence of the Spirit in our lives (Acts 2:38–39), and by walking in the Spirit we receive gifts and bear fruit (Gal. 5:22–23). Simeon received the gift of wisdom and awareness that the Messiah would come in his lifetime. A gift that the Spirit may give us is wisdom and understanding. The Spirit reveals God's wisdom to us. Through the help of the Spirit we are able to grow a true knowledge of God (1 Cor. 2:10–13).

~

The Spirit Prepares Jesus for Ministry

from Matthew 3:13–17

John, the son of Zechariah and Elizabeth, grew up and moved away from his parents' home, choosing to live alone in the desert of Judea. By the time he was thirty years old he was spiritually strong and had started preaching to the people that the Messiah was coming soon. Crowds of people traveled from their towns and cities into the desert to hear John teach. When they believed what he said, John baptized them in the water of the Jordan River. Eventually John, son of Zechariah, became known as John the Baptist.

One day Jesus left his home in Nazareth and walked many miles to find John near the Jordan

River. As he approached the riverbank, Jesus called out to John, "John, I'm glad I found you. I need you to baptize me."

"That can't be," John replied. "I can't baptize you. You should be baptizing me. So why are you here?"

"But this needs to be done," Jesus insisted. "We need to do this because God wants you to baptize me. We don't need any other reason."

As soon as Jesus was baptized, he went up out of the water. At that moment heaven was opened, and he saw the Spirit of God descending like a dove and alighting on him. (Matthew 3:16)

John finally agreed. The two men waded into the river, and John proceeded to baptize Jesus with water from the river. As Jesus began to wade toward the shore, he lifted his head up and looked toward the sky. Suddenly heaven opened; the Holy Spirit glided down out of the sky like a dove, hovered near Jesus, and gently settled on his shoulder. Immediately a voice boomed from heaven, declaring: "You are my Son, whom I dearly love. I am pleased with you. You are my pleasure and my joy."

Then Jesus walked out of the river full of the

Spirit and the affirmation of his Father. Now he was equipped to begin his ministry to the people. He was prepared with the power of the Spirit to heal the sick, make blind people see and deaf people hear, and cause crippled people to walk. He would not only feed and heal people, he would free them from their demons, forgive their sins, and shower God's love on everyone.

The Spirit Today

The Spirit's presence is acknowledged today through the sacrament of baptism, as we are baptized "in the name of the Father, the Son, and the Holy Spirit" just as Christ commanded his disciples to baptize all nations (Matt. 28:19). Through baptism we are prepared to live a life for Christ. The Spirit claims us and declares us to be God's children: "The Spirit himself testifies with our spirit that we are God's children. Now if we are children, then we are heirs—heirs of God and co-heirs with Christ" (Rom. 8:16–17). We are also baptized by one Spirit into one body of Christ (1 Cor. 12:13).

In addition, pastors are called to ministry through a service of ordination in which the Spirit's presence is acknowledged. Their calling to ministry may be a private event, but the ceremony of ordination is a more public recognition and acknowledgment of the Spirit's powerful work in a minister's life.

———

The Spirit Helps Nicodemus Believe

from John 3:1–21

The Jewish leaders called Pharisees despised Jesus because he claimed to be the Son of God. Not only did that kind of talk make them uncomfortable, it made them downright furious with this new teacher. Nicodemus, however, felt different, even though he himself was a Pharisee. Eager to learn more about Jesus' message, Nicodemus came to talk to Jesus in the dark of night, when no one would see him. He was curious about Jesus and what he had been preaching, but he didn't want to incite the anger of the Pharisees.

"Rabbi," Nicodemus said to Jesus, "we know God sent you here to be a teacher. No one can do the things you do if God is not with them."

"You are right," Jesus answered. "And no one can enter the kingdom of God without being born again."

"How does that happen?" Nicodemus asked. "Can a grown person go back to being an infant inside its mother's womb a second time?"

The wind blows wherever it pleases. You hear its sound, but you cannot tell where it comes from or where it is going. So it is with everyone born of the Spirit. (John 3:8)

"No, that's not exactly what I mean," Jesus replied. "You can enter the Kingdom of God only by being born of the Spirit and water. Humans can give birth only to humans. But the Spirit gives birth to things that are spiritual. The Spirit blows like the wind— wherever it wants to. We don't know where it comes from or where it's going. We also don't know where the Spirit will stop and to whom he will give new life."

"I still don't understand," Nicodemus confessed.

"You are a teacher and you still don't understand what I'm saying?" Jesus asked. "Here's the truth: I know what I'm talking about, and so do my disciples. We are all certain of all the things we've witnessed. But I know that you don't want to accept what we're saying. If you don't believe me about things you *can* see, how will you believe me about things in heaven that you can't see? Only the Son of Man, who came from heaven, has seen heaven. Everyone who believes in him and what he says will live in fellowship with God, now and forever."

Eventually Nicodemus understood everything Jesus had told him. The Holy Spirit inspired Nicodemus to believe in Jesus, gave him new life, and transformed Nicodemus's thoughts and actions. Through the power of the Spirit, Nicodemus was born again and given a new life in Christ.

The Spirit Today

Nicodemus heard the facts, but they didn't make sense to him. The concept of being born again was completely foreign to his usual way of thinking. Coming to a full realization and understanding of rebirth required the power of the Spirit. Like Abraham, who by faith believed in the promises of God through the Spirit, so too Nicodemus came to faith. The Spirit works in us and in others the same way he did for Abraham, Nicodemus, and the early church. Through the Spirit's power we come to believe what our minds cannot reason and our hearts resist.

Although the story doesn't include the exact account of Nicodemus coming to faith, we do have proof that this change occurred. Years later Nicodemus defended Jesus when other Pharisees mocked him (John 7:50–52), and after Jesus died, Nicodemus assisted in removing his body, preparing it for burial, and placing him in a tomb (John 19:38–42).

―

The Spirit Will Come and Stay Forever

from John 14

For three years Jesus traveled all over Israel, preaching, teaching, healing and helping people. As his ministry was coming to an end and his death was approaching, Jesus yearned to spend more time with his disciples. In order to do so, Jesus invited his twelve disciples to share a supper in celebration of Passover to remember God's freeing his people from slavery in Egypt.

When Jesus and his disciples were settled around the table, Jesus started talking. "I need to explain something to you now, while we're still together. I'm going away soon to return to my Father, but don't worry, you won't be left alone. My Father will send a helper called the Spirit of Truth who will never leave you. Most people in the world don't know him because they don't believe in him, but you already know him because he lives with you and in you. Because you have been with me faithfully from the beginning of my ministry, you have knowledge of the truth and will begin sharing that truth with others. The helper, the Holy Spirit, will teach you everything you need for ministry and will remind you of everything I've ever said."

> "But the Advocate, the Holy Spirit, whom the Father will send in my name, will teach you all things and will remind you of everything I have said to you." (John 14:26)

The disciples were overwhelmed and puzzled. "Why do you have to go away?" they asked. "Stay with us!"

"I know you don't want me to leave," Jesus replied, "and I know you're really sad because I've told you I'm leaving, but it's a good thing that I'm going away. If I don't go, the Holy Spirit won't come to you. But if I go, I promise I'll send the Holy Spirit to you."

Jesus continued to reassure his followers. "Remember that I love you," he said. "I've loved you the way the Father has loved me, and here's what I want you to do—live in love. Love each other."

When Jesus finished talking, he lifted his face toward heaven and prayed. Then he and his disciples sang a song to conclude their time together. As they finished singing they got up from the table, descended the stairs, and walked across the city to the garden of Gethsemane on the Mount of Olives.

The Spirit Today

We are guaranteed the presence of the Spirit if we believe and are baptized (Eph. 1:13–14). The Spirit's presence as the Comforter will be with us. How often we forget that the promise of God's presence through the Spirit was not just a promise from Jesus to his disciples so long ago, but a promise to us as well. We should live in the hope and the joy of the Spirit that lives within us. Start each day by focusing on the Spirit's presence in your life. Meditate and find comfort in the promise of God's Spirit living in his people. Make an effort to witness the Spirit living in your life and in the lives of others around you.

The Spirit Resurrects Jesus

from John 19:38–42, 20:1–21; I Peter 3:18

> For Christ also suffered once for sins, the righteous
> for the unrighteous, to bring you to God. He was
> put to death in the body but made alive in the Spirit.
> (I Peter 3:18)

Knowing he was going to die soon, Jesus escorted his
disciples to the garden of Gethsemane for a time of
prayer. Jesus didn't want to endure the horrible death
that awaited him; he consulted God in prayer, asking if
God could alter the impending event. As Jesus finished
praying, the Roman soldiers marched into the garden,
seized Jesus, and arrested him. Although he had done
nothing wrong, Jesus was declared guilty during a brief
trial and sentenced to death. He was crucified on a
cross—a horrible and painful punishment—and died.
Then Nicodemus and a man named Joseph claimed
Jesus' body, prepared it for burial, and laid it in a tomb.
To ensure no one could enter the grave and steal Jesus'
body, the two men secured the burial site by placing a
huge stone in front of the entrance. They left the site to
grieve the loss of their teacher and readjust their thinking to living without him.

They had no idea that Jesus' death and burial weren't the end. God had a fabulous plan for a new beginning. Through the work of the Holy Spirit, the great Giver and Renewer of Life, Jesus would come alive again!

Unfortunately Jesus' friends didn't remember he had said he would come alive again. They stayed together to mourn Jesus' death on Friday night, all day Saturday, and into Sunday morning. Before dawn on Sunday morning, Mary from the town of Magdala left the city to visit Jesus' tomb. She was determined to check the body and add more spices to mask the stench of the decaying flesh. When Mary neared the tomb, she noticed the large stone in front had been moved off to the side. The tomb was wide open...and empty! Mary was shocked and frightened because Jesus' body had disappeared. Uncertain of what to do next, she hurried back into the city and found Peter and John.

"He's not there!" she shouted. "Somebody has taken Jesus out of the tomb, and I don't know where they put him!"

Peter and John ran back to the tomb to see for themselves. They went into the tomb and found the cloths that had been wrapped around Jesus' body. But his body was no longer there—it was gone! Not certain of what to do, they returned to the place in the city where they were staying.

Meanwhile Mary stood outside the tomb crying. She looked once more into the tomb that she thought was empty, but this time she saw something! Two bright and shining white angels rested on the stone slab where Jesus' body had been.

"Why are you crying?" they asked Mary.

"They've taken away Jesus, my Lord, and I don't know where they have put him," she replied.

Then Mary turned around. And right in front of her stood Jesus. Mary had no idea who the figure in front of her was.

"Why are you crying? What are you looking for?" Jesus asked.

Thinking the person in front of her was the gardener, Mary replied, "If you've taken him away, tell me where you've put him and I'll go get him."

Then Jesus said just one word, "Mary."

And suddenly Mary knew—this was Jesus, her Lord, her teacher and friend. He wasn't dead; he had come back to life! Mary joyfully ran to Jesus to hug him, but he stopped her and said, "Don't hold on to me. I haven't ascended to the Father. Quick, go back to my disciples and tell them I'm alive."

Mary did as Jesus said and told the disciples the

good news. "Jesus is alive. I've seen him and talked with him. He is risen!" Then she told them everything Jesus had said.

The impossible had happened. But as we learned in other stories where old women have babies, and a sea divides in two, and victory in battle comes without bloodshed, nothing is impossible for God. Through the power of the Holy Spirit, the Lord and Giver of Life, Jesus had been raised back to life from the dead.

The Spirit Today

Jesus suffered and died to save sinners from God's anger and punishment. He came alive again by the power of the Holy Spirit. His resurrection is a testimony to us that he has conquered death, and just as he was raised from the dead, we too will rise again some day. What the Holy Spirit did for Jesus, he will do for us as well, renewing and restoring us from death and raising us to eternal life. "He saved us through the washing of rebirth and renewal by the Holy Spirit, whom he poured out on us generously through Jesus Christ our Savior, so that, having been justified by his grace, we might become heirs having the hope of eternal life" (Titus 3:5–7). "And if the Spirit of him who raised Jesus from the dead is living in you, he who raised Christ from the dead will also give life to your mortal bodies because of his Spirit who lives in you" (Rom. 8:11).

—

The Holy Spirit Comes at Pentecost

from Acts 1:1–11, 2:1–41

One day when the resurrected Jesus and his disciples were on the Mount of Olives, Jesus told them, "Go back to Jerusalem and stay there a few days until my Father sends you what he has promised. John the Baptist baptized everyone with water, but you will be baptized with the Holy Spirit. The Spirit will give you power to tell others about me. Share the good news with the people in Jerusalem first, then spread the word to everyone in Judea and Samaria, and finally travel throughout the world. Go everywhere, baptize the people who believe, then teach them everything I've taught you while I was here on earth."

As Jesus finished speaking, he suddenly rose up into the sky, disappeared behind a cloud, and was received into heaven. After watching this stunning event, Jesus' disciples returned to Jerusalem and stayed together, as Jesus had instructed them to do. They spent the next week in earnest prayer as they waited for the Helper who Jesus had promised would come.

Jerusalem was crowded with people because it was festival week in celebration of the Festival of Harvest. Jewish people from other countries had come to Jerusalem to celebrate. On the day of Pentecost the disciples and followers of Jesus were together in one room when suddenly they heard a strange noise, something they had never heard before; it was similar to the sound of a strong wind rushing through the trees, and echoed through the whole house. Then tongues made of fire appeared and flickered over the head of each person in the room. The Holy Spirit had come, filling every person in the room with his power! Immediately each person started talking in a language they had never spoken before.

All of them were filled with the Holy Spirit and began to speak in other tongues as the Spirit enabled them. (Acts 2:4)

When the crowds of Jews heard the noises coming from the house, they gathered outside in the street to listen. They were surprised to hear people speaking various foreign languages. Different people from a variety of nations could actually understand every word spoken.

"How do these people know so many different languages?" the foreigners asked each other. "Aren't they all from Galilee?"

"Maybe they're drunk," someone said, making fun of the disciples.

Overhearing what the foreigners said, Peter left the house, came outside to face the crowd, and addressed them boldly: "No, we haven't been drinking wine. This is the big event God's prophets wrote about. The Spirit has come—the Spirit that Joel the prophet talked about when he said, 'This is what God says, "I will pour out my Spirit on everyone, both men and women. They will tell others what God has shown them. On that day whoever calls on the name of the Lord will be saved." ' This is the day of that prophecy's fulfillment. That same Spirit has come!"

When the people heard this, they asked Peter, "What should we do?"

Peter answered, "All of you must turn to God. Change the way you think, live, and act. Believe in Jesus and be baptized so that your sins will be forgiven. Then you too will receive the gift of the Holy

Spirit. This promise is true for you, your families, and everyone all over the world."

That same day about three thousand people believed what Peter said. They were baptized and joined the growing group of Christians.

At the end of the day, when the speeches were over and everyone was baptized, the Spirit didn't leave. Instead he stayed with every person he had filled. In the days of the Old Testament, the Spirit came only for a short time to help someone get a special job done; then he would leave. Now everything was different. Just as the Spirit had come and stayed with Jesus for his entire life, he would come and stay forever with everyone who believed.

The Spirit Today

The church's birthday is the day on which the Holy Spirit descended onto the disciples who were gathered together in prayer. This is a day of great significance in the church, yet we all but ignore the occasion. Every year, about seven weeks after Easter (fifty days from Easter Sunday, in accordance with the meaning of the word *Pentecost*, fiftieth day), Pentecost arrives. Just as the disciples received the power of the Spirit on this day, we too receive the Spirit's power when we become believers. This power ensures that the word of salvation will be preached throughout the world, that we will be witnesses of God's love and grace. The Spirit provides us with the strength to testify, to preach and teach, to love. Through his power we have the strength to face evil and to be bold in precarious or threatening situations. The coming of the power of the Spirit is worth our notice, commemoration, and celebration. This year mark your calendar and spend some time on the fiftieth day after Easter in celebration of the Spirit's coming—both the first coming to the church and the day that you yourself received the Spirit.

Chapter Six

The Spirit's Work Continues

"Natural man needs the Holy Spirit in his life if he
is to become capable of doing spiritual good."

Edwin H. Palmer

As Jesus was preparing to leave the earth, he promised
his disciples that he would not desert them; rather he
would send the Spirit, the Comforter and Teacher,
to be with them. Now the Spirit was going to take
center stage—to explode into the lives of individuals, to empower them to spread the Good News, to
inspire the message presented, to guide their travels
and establish communities of churches "in all Judea
and Samaria, and to the ends of the earth" (Acts
1:8). He would put a new heart and a new spirit in all
believers. And he will stay with us until God finishes
his work in us. The Spirit promised by the prophets

centuries before was coming, not only to change individuals but to change the world.

—

The Holy Spirit Fills the Samaritans

from Acts 8:4–25

After receiving the Holy Spirit, one of Jesus' disciples, named Philip, left Jerusalem. He traveled north to the city of Samaria to preach about Jesus to the people. In the name of Jesus he performed many miracles: he healed paralyzed people and helped them move again. He made lame people walk and commanded evil spirits to depart from victims. Crowds of people gathered to hear his message and witness the miracles.

A man named Simon lived in Samaria when Philip arrived to preach. Simon was a sorcerer who claimed he was the greatest magician ever. Men and women, boys and girls were amazed by his magic tricks. In fact, the people thought that Simon had the power of God and called him the Great Power of God. But they soon realized they were wrong when Philip came to town. Philip preached about Jesus and performed for them the greatest miracles they had ever seen. They believed what Philip said and were baptized. Simon the sorcerer, fascinated with Philip's words and actions, followed him everywhere.

Soon after Peter and John heard that the Samaritans had accepted the Good News of Jesus, they hurried to Samaria and prayed that the people would receive the gift of the Holy Spirit. As soon as Peter's and John's hands touched the people, the Holy Spirit filled the Samaritans with power.

When Simon the sorcerer watched Peter and John lay their hands on the people and give them the Spirit, he thought, *What a wonderful and powerful trick that is! I must have it to add to my show.* Approaching the two disciples, Simon said, "That was a powerful performance. I want to do that too. Here, take this money in exchange for that special power you have. Then I can touch people like you do and magically give them the Spirit."

"Keep your money," Peter said angrily. "You can't buy the Holy Spirit like a magic trick—it's a free gift from God alone. Go away, Simon, you can't be involved in our ministry. God will destroy both you and your money because of your twisted mind. Here's my advice—get rid of your wicked thoughts and ask God to forgive you for even thinking such things."

Simon was suddenly afraid of the threat that God would destroy him. He pleaded with Peter, "If that's true, then pray for me that nothing happens."

Then Peter and John left the city of Samaria and in the power of the Holy Spirit continued to spread the Good News that Jesus was the Messiah.

The Spirit Today

Like Simon, people today are often attracted to Christians who seem to have it all together. Perhaps they see something in such people's lives that they want—peace of mind, happiness, a wholeness that's hard to describe. They just know the other person has something, and they want it too. They may even think that if they pay a fee or sign up for it, as if it were a bottled lotion or a gym membership, they too can reap the rewards and benefits. Eventually, however, they probably realize, as Simon did, that those qualities can't be paid for, they're not for sale, they are free. No one can buy what the Spirit offers. The benefits of having faith in Jesus are a free gift. By faith we receive salvation through Jesus and all the benefits of living in the Spirit: assurance that we are God's children (Gal. 4:6); new life (2 Cor. 3:6), freedom (2 Cor. 3:17), and strength (Eph. 3:16). The Spirit will also pray for us (Rom. 8:26), give us access to the Father (Eph. 2:18), and provide us with gifts (1 Cor. 12:4–11). All of these things are free to anyone who believes.

~

The Spirit Illuminates the Word

from Acts 8:26–39

After preaching in Samaria, Philip received a message from one of God's angels. "Leave Samaria and travel south using the desert road that connects Jerusalem to Gaza," the angel told him. That simple instruction was the entire message the angel provided. Philip didn't receive an explanation as to why he should go, how he should travel, or what he would find along the way. But without asking any questions Philip departed Samaria, traveled to Jerusalem, and started walking on the road to Gaza. Soon he spotted a chariot in the distance parked on the side of the road.

The Holy Spirit nudged Philip and told him, "See that chariot? Go over to it and stand there." Philip ran up to the chariot and heard a man reading Scripture from the book of Isaiah the prophet. The man who was reading was an important official from Ethiopia in charge of all the treasures of the queen. He had been to Jerusalem to worship God in the Temple and was now on his way home.

"Do you understand what you are reading?" Philip asked the Ethiopian.

"How can I?" the man replied. "I don't have anyone to explain it to me. Come up here and sit with me for a while."

So Philip climbed into the chariot and sat down as the Ethiopian read these words: "He was led like a sheep to the slaughter, and as a lamb before its shearer is silent, so he did not open his mouth."

"Who's the prophet talking about?" the official asked. "Is he talking about himself or someone else?"

Philip began to explain the passage to the Ethiopian while they rode together in the chariot. He told him that Isaiah was referring to Jesus the Messiah. Philip continued the lesson, providing additional information on how Jesus had come to earth and died to save people from their sins.

As the chariot passed a pond on the side of the road, the official said to Philip, "Look, there's water over there. Can I be baptized?" After the official ordered his driver to pull the chariot off the road, he and Philip climbed down from the chariot and walked into the water. Then Philip said, "I baptize you in the name of the Father and the Son and the Holy Spirit." As soon as the men walked out of the water, the Spirit of God suddenly whisked Philip away. Much as he had transported Ezekiel, the Spirit removed Philip from the scene without noise or motion. Philip simply disappeared!

Although his friend had vanished, the Ethiopian official returned to his chariot and resumed his journey. He was full of joy over all that had happened. But he never saw Philip again.

The Spirit Today

The Ethiopian was able to read the words of Isaiah, but the meaning eluded him. Through the Spirit's work in Philip and in the Ethiopian, the words were illuminated and contained true meaning and purpose, transforming the reader from an unbeliever to a believer. "All Scripture is God-breathed and is useful for teaching, rebuking, correcting and training in righteousness" (2 Tim. 3:16).

The Spirit illuminates our understanding of what God's message says to us today. We may read the words of the Bible or hear them read to us in a worship service, but it is only through the power and the illumination of the Spirit that we begin to understand and apply the meaning of those words to our hearts and lives. Anyone can read a passage from the Bible, but without the work of the Spirit, the words are merely that—words on a page without meaning, without worth. It is the Spirit's power in us that makes those black letters on a white page change our minds and our lives. Through the Spirit's illumination, we receive understanding and comfort and peace from the word of God. Through the work of the Spirit those words become the very power of God (Rom. 1:16) that changes lives, brings comfort and peace, moves someone to tears or to action. The next time you read the Bible or hear it read at a church service, listen intently, remember that the Spirit is at work, and be receptive to his powerful work within you.

The Holy Spirit Transforms Saul

from Acts 9:1–22

Under the guidance of the Spirit the new Christians eagerly spread the news about Jesus in spite of the attempts of a zealous Jewish man named Saul to stop them. Saul was furious that anyone could believe something other than Jewish laws, Jewish teaching, and the accepted methods of worship. He threatened to murder anyone who talked about Jesus as the Messiah and was determined to annihilate all those who believed in him. He even asked the priests from the Temple in Jerusalem to write letters to the synagogue leaders in Damascus commanding that anyone claiming to be a Christian be arrested and thrown into prison. He himself planned to go to Damascus, hunt down the Christians, put them in chains, and drag them back to Jerusalem. However, on his journey something happened that not only changed Saul's plans but also changed the entire world!

As Saul and his group approached Damascus around noontime, a light from heaven suddenly flashed around Saul. The light was brighter than the summer sun and forced Saul to fall down on the ground to protect himself.

Then a voice from heaven called out, "Saul, Saul, why are you so against me? Why are you harassing my people?"

"Who are you?" Saul asked.

The voice replied, "I am Jesus. The one you are persecuting. Now get up and enter the city. You'll be told what to do when you get there."

Saul rose to his feet and opened his eyes. He suddenly realized—he couldn't see. The light had blinded him! His traveling companions came to his aid, taking him by the hand and leading him into the city. They found Saul a room in a house on Straight Street and left him there. For three days Saul stayed in his room. He didn't eat; he didn't drink; he didn't do anything, because he couldn't see.

Meanwhile, in another part of the city, a man named Ananias had a vision from God. In his vision God told Ananias, "Go to Judas's house on Straight Street. Look for a man named Saul. He knows you're coming, and you'll help him see again."

"But Lord," Ananias protested, "Saul is evil and dangerous. He wants to throw people in jail who follow Jesus."

"Just go!" God answered. "Saul is special to me. I've chosen him to bring my name to the nations, to leaders and kings, as well as to the Jews. He will suffer a lot for me."

Then Ananias went to the house and entered it. Placing his hands on Saul, he said, "Brother Saul, the Lord—Jesus, who appeared to you on the road as you were coming here—has sent me so that you may see again and be filled with the Holy Spirit." (Acts 9:17)

Ananias left his home, headed to Straight Street, entered Judas's house, and found Saul sitting in his room. As Ananias placed his hands on Saul, he said, "Brother Saul, the Lord—Jesus, who stopped you on the road—sent me here. He wants you to see again and be filled with the Holy Spirit." Immediately white flakes like fish scales fell from Saul's eyes, and his eyesight was restored. Saul stood up, and Ananias baptized him. Just as the Spirit had filled other believers at their baptism, the Spirit filled Saul, preparing him to preach the name of Jesus.

Later Saul met with the other disciples in Damascus. Then he visited the Jewish synagogues and started preaching that Jesus was the Son of God, the long-awaited Messiah. Everyone who heard him was amazed that Saul, once evil and dangerous, had been radically changed into a powerful preacher for Jesus.

The Spirit Today

The Holy Spirit does more than reform lives; he completely transforms them. No one is beyond the Spirit's powerful grasp or immune to his influence, no matter how sinful that person's life may be. Even Saul's hatred and anger could not resist the Spirit's power. Saul, a malicious murderer who wrecked havoc in the lives of the new Christians, made a complete turnaround and became a zealous preacher of Christ by the work of the Spirit. If the Spirit was capable of completely transforming the life of someone like that, he certainly is capable of handling anyone. When we receive the Spirit, he will transform us into new life, instilling in us the ability to become more like God: "We all, who with unveiled faces contemplate the Lord's glory, are being transformed into his image with ever-increasing glory, which comes from the Lord, who is the Spirit" (2 Cor. 3:18). Each day take a moment to focus on the sanctifying work of the Spirit. How is the Spirit working in your life? How do you see yourself becoming more Christlike?

⌣

The Holy Spirit Is Available to Everyone

from Acts 10:9–46

While the apostle Peter was visiting the city of Joppa, he climbed up to a rooftop to be alone and pray. As he relaxed in the warm afternoon sun and dozed, he saw the sky open up and a big white linen bedsheet float down to the ground. Peter could see that the sheet was full of all kinds of animals, reptiles, and birds.

A voice called out to him, "Peter! Get up. Kill the animals you see and eat them."

"But Lord," Peter replied, "some of these animals are classified untouchable by Jewish law. They're the ones you've told us never to eat because they are impure and unclean. I've never touched any of them, much less eaten these kinds of creatures. Only non-Jewish people do that."

"You shouldn't say such things, Peter," the voice answered. "God has made *all* these animals clean." Then the voice was silent, and the sheet drifted away.

A while later the sheet drifted down again, the

animals appeared, and the voice from heaven repeated the conversation with Peter. Then the sheet loaded with creatures vanished. The performance was repeated a third time: the sheet of creatures floated down from the sky, a voice from heaven talked to Peter, he replied, then the animals in the sheet disappeared. Eventually Peter woke up and left the rooftop, but he kept thinking about his vision. He was puzzled as to what it all could mean.

Meanwhile, in the city of Caesarea, an angel of God appeared to a military officer named Cornelius who loved God, prayed to him, and often supported the poor people in his city. The angel told Cornelius, "Send some of your men to Joppa to find Peter and bring him here."

The same day that Peter had his unusual vision, three men sent by Cornelius came to the city asking for Peter. They found the house where Peter was staying and waited outside. Meanwhile Peter was upstairs trying to figure out the meaning of the vision. Suddenly the air moved, and the Holy Spirit entered the room.

"Peter, three men are looking for you," the Spirit said. "They are outside waiting. Go downstairs and follow their instructions. Don't be afraid to go with them, because I've sent them to get you."

Peter did exactly as the Spirit instructed. The next day he traveled with the three men to Caesarea to meet Cornelius. Knowing that Peter's coming was important, Cornelius had made big plans for his arrival. He'd invited his friends and relatives to come over to his house to greet Peter when he arrived.

When Peter entered Cornelius's house and saw all the non-Jewish people there, he suddenly knew what the vision from God meant: all animals were the same now, all were clean, all were pure, all were acceptable; and in the same way all people were acceptable to God. God sees everyone the same—Jews and non-Jews, men and women, military officers and regular citizens, enslaved and free people. People may be different in the eyes of people, but not in the eyes of God.

Then Peter said to the crowd, "Now I understand what God was trying to tell me in this vision I had a few days ago. God doesn't show favoritism when it comes to people. He accepts anyone who respects him and does what is right. God sent Jesus to the Jews first, to bring them the news that he has forgiven their sins. But now I see that Jesus came with the Good News for everyone, not just the Jews. He is *everyone's* Lord."

> While Peter was still speaking these words, the Holy Spirit came on all who heard the message. The circumcised believers who had come with Peter were astonished that the gift of the Holy Spirit had been poured out even on Gentiles. (Acts 10:44–45)

While Peter was telling the crowd about Jesus, the Holy Spirit came and filled them with his power. The Jewish believers who accompanied Peter were amazed that the Holy Spirit had rested on the people who were not Jewish! This had never happened before. Then the non-Jewish people started speaking in other languages and praising God. They sang songs and danced with jubilance because they were filled with the Holy Spirit.

The Spirit Today

Peter had always believed in the Jewish tradition that God's favor was for the Jews only. Outsiders of the time (Gentiles and Samaritans) were not welcome to receive God's grace or salvation. All that changed through Peter's vision and realization: "God does not show favoritism but accepts from every nation the one who fears him and does what is right"

(Acts 10:34–35). His conclusion was confirmed by the Spirit's arrival on everyone who was listening (Acts 10:44).

The Spirit's invitation to live a life of wholeness, joy, and peace is not limited to a select group, race, ethnicity, or gender. A Spirit-filled life is available to all people, in the present and in the future. In the present the Spirit comes without limit (John 3:34), and it will remain with us forever (John 14:16–17). In the future the Spirit will extend an invitation to everyone at the end of time, calling to all to receive the gift of life: "The Spirit and the bride say, 'Come!' And let the one who hears say, 'Come!' Let the one who is thirsty come; and let the one who wishes take the free gift of the water of life" (Rev. 22:17).

The Spirit Expands the Church

from Acts 13:1–12

Under the guidance of the Spirit, the apostles had spread the Good News in the order Jesus had directed—through Judea and Samaria, west into

Phoenicia and the island of Cyprus, and north to Syria. But now the Spirit was calling them to fulfill the last part of Christ's command to go into all the world and preach the Good News to all creation. The church was ready to branch out into new territories under the direction and power of the Holy Spirit.

> While they were worshiping the Lord and fasting, the Holy Spirit said, "Set apart for me Barnabas and Saul for the work to which I have called them." (Acts 13:2)

Through the power of the Spirit, the Christian church grew in the city of Antioch, Syria. Barnabas, Simeon, Lucius, Manaen, and Saul, the church leaders, had received the Spirit's gifts of prophecy and teaching. Saul, who was also called Paul, was among those with these special gifts. One day as they gathered together, the Holy Spirit spoke to the group. "Barnabas and Paul need to leave this group and go off to preach elsewhere," he said. Although the directive was plain and simple, the five men were uncertain of the details, so they spent some time fasting and praying to focus on what should be done. Soon they realized that Barnabas and Paul needed to leave the church in Antioch and go off to the island of

Cyprus and then into the regions of Asia and Galatia to preach, to teach, and to establish new churches. Shortly before the two left, Simeon, Lucius, and Manaen placed their hands on Barnabas and Paul, blessing them for safe travels and for their future mission work.

> The two of them, sent on their way by the Holy Spirit, went down to Seleucia and sailed from there to Cyprus. (Acts 13:4)

The Holy Spirit was with Barnabas and Paul as they left Antioch with John Mark as their helper. The three traveled to the port city of Seleucia on the coast of the Mediterranean Sea, where they boarded a sailing ship headed west to the island of Cyprus. The trip was uneventful, and Barnabas and Paul were able to preach the Good News of Jesus in the local Jewish synagogues upon arriving in Salamis, Cyprus. Encouraged by the Holy Spirit, they traveled throughout the island, preaching in every town. People listened to them, but nothing noteworthy happened along the way until they arrived in the city of Paphos. Almost immediately they ran into a man who was suspicious of them and their message.

Bar-Jesus (also called Elymas) was a Jewish false

prophet, a sorcerer, and a personal attendant to the governor, Sergius Paulus. Bar-Jesus opposed the preaching of Paul and Barnabas and tried to influence the governor. But Sergius Paulus was an intelligent man who was curious about the word of God. Knowing that Paul and Barnabas were in the city, he sent for them in spite of the objections from his attendant.

As Barnabas and Paul arrived at the governor's palace, they heard Elymas arguing with the governor and speaking against their visit. His opposition was ruthless, which Paul found offensive. Filled with the power of the Holy Spirit, Paul boldly approached Elymas, looked him directly in the eye, and said, "Elymas, you are the son of the devil, the enemy of all truth and goodness. Your blood runs thick with deceit and trickery. Stop perverting God's goodness and how he wants us to live. You have definitely gone too far this time. God is against you, and you're going to be so blind you won't be able to see the light of day."

Immediately Elymas couldn't see. Mist and darkness enveloped him, making him grope about. He waved his hands, trying to find his way around, and begged for someone to assist him. Meanwhile Sergius Paulus watched in amazement and was stunned by the suddenness of Elymas's transformation. He had listened carefully to Paul's reprimand and his teaching about God, and now there was no doubt in his mind; he believed in the word of God and everything Paul had said.

The Spirit Today

Without the power of the Holy Spirit, the leaders of the early church would have struggled to spread the news about Jesus. The logistics of travel were daunting, members disagreed and argued over process and procedure, Jewish beliefs were firmly established, and Roman emperor worship permeated the empire. Realistically it would have been impossible to introduce a radically new way of thinking to the world, but the apostles did not have to do the work on their own strength or personal charisma; the very power of God Almighty was with them. The power of the Spirit told them where to go (Acts 16:6–10) and what to say (Acts 4:8; 13:9); he eliminated obstacles (Acts 13:11–12) and encouraged them (Acts 9:31).

The Spirit continues to build up the church through the life of each of its members. "And in him you too are being built together to become a dwelling in which God lives by his Spirit" (Eph. 2:22). The Spirit still leads, still directs, still speaks. No one and nothing can stop the Spirit from spreading the Good News throughout the world.

—

The Spirit Provides Gifts and Yields Fruit

from I Corinthians 12, Galatians 5

Paul was a great preacher who traveled throughout the Mediterranean world telling others about Jesus. He established numerous churches, but while the churches were still new, Paul delegated the responsibilities of growing the church to someone else, and moved on to another city to establish yet another church. Paul, however, didn't forget the Christians in the newly established churches; he wrote letters full of encouragement and instruction to help them grow in their faith and in their understanding of the Holy Spirit.

Paul wrote to the Christian church in Corinth, Greece, to provide them with information about the work of the Holy Spirit in the lives of believers. He explained that the Spirit gives special gifts to each individual.

> There are different kinds of gifts, but the same Spirit distributes them. (I Corinthians 12:4)

To God's Church in Corinth,

I always thank God for you because he has shown his good will toward you and called you to be partners with his Son Jesus Christ.

Stay united in your understanding and opinions about the Spirit and the gifts he has given you. Above all, remember that the Spirit gives different gifts and abilities to different individuals. But all of these gifts come from the exact same source— the Holy Spirit. He provides gifts as evidence that he is present with us. He disperses a variety of gifts so that everyone will benefit from them. To some he gives wisdom or knowledge as well as the ability to share it with others. He gives courageous faith to some people and to others he gives the ability to heal the sick. Others can perform miracles or reveal God's secrets. Some people can discern types of spirits, while still others have the gift of speaking various languages or interpreting those languages.

There are many gifts but only one Spirit, who provides something different to each person. The Spirit-provided gifts vary from person to person, but together the variety of gifts benefit the entire body of Christ—the church.

If you're having trouble understanding this, think about the human body. The body is one unit, one whole, and yet it has many parts. Each part has a different function, but every part works in coordination with the others. The foot doesn't say to the hand, "I'm not a hand, so I'm not part of the body." Nor does the eye say, "I'm not an ear, so I'm not part of the body." God put the body together with various parts, each of which performs a special function for the good of the whole body. As there are many parts to the body, so there are many parts to the church—the body of Christ. Each of you has a special gift to provide for the function of the whole.

Don't argue over who has the better gifts, for the greatest gift of all is love.

May the grace of the Lord Jesus Christ be with you all.

Love, Paul

Paul also wrote a letter to the Christian churches in the area of Galatia (modern-day Turkey) to explain to the believers that if the Spirit lives actively in their lives, they will witness the results by displaying the fruit of the Spirit.

The fruit of the Spirit is love, joy, peace, forbearance, kindness, goodness, faithfulness, gentleness and self-control. (Galatians 5:22–23)

My dear brothers and sisters in the churches of Galatia,

May God's peace be with you. I've heard you are confused and have already forgotten what I told you. Don't be stupid! Don't listen to those false teachers. What I told you about Jesus is absolutely the truth. The Holy Spirit came to you freely because of your faith in Jesus, not because of your own efforts to follow the rules and regulations of the Jewish law. Don't revert to that old way of thinking. Stay focused and believe what I told you about Jesus.

Stay away from evil, and resist your natural desire to sin. If you follow the Spirit, your lives will display the results of living for Jesus. Those results are called fruit. The fruits of the Spirit are love, joy, peace, patience, kindness, goodness, faithfulness, gentleness, and self-control. Since we live by the Spirit, let's make sure we stay close to the Spirit. If you do things that please the Spirit, you will receive eternal life.

May the good will of our Lord and Savior Jesus Christ be with you all.

Paul, a servant of Jesus

The Spirit Today

The world and all its glitz and glamor may manipulate us into believing that we can secure peace and find joy in things, power, or position; but true peace and genuine joy come only from the Spirit living within us. Living in the Spirit is a way of life. It is a holistic lifestyle that God desires for us as we work to bring about his kingdom here on earth as it is in heaven. "For the kingdom of God is not a matter of eating and drinking, but of righteousness, peace and joy in the Holy Spirit" (Rom. 14:17). Living in the joy and peace of the Spirit can be a reality no matter what controversies or wars are raging in the world or what drama is presenting itself on social media or in the news. As Christians, we are reminded: "Since we live by the Spirit, let us keep in step with the Spirit" (Gal. 5:25). By being full of the Spirit we will share in the gifts of the Spirit as well as display his fruit.

"Teach me to do your will, for you are my God;
may your good Spirit lead me on level ground."

Psalms 143:10

Acknowledgments

I would like to acknowledge my professors at Calvin Theological Seminary who first introduced me to the work of the Holy Spirit and aroused my curiosity about the third person of the Trinity. The seeds they planted while I was a student took root as I researched the topic on my own after graduation and eventually bloomed into this book. Much thanks also goes to my editor, Adrienne Ingrum, who believed in the rough manuscript long before I did and continued to encourage me through its various revisions.

About the Author

DORIS WYNBEEK RIKKERS has worked in Christian publishing for more than forty years and was managing editor of the team that originally published the New International Version of the Bible (NIV)—the most widely read contemporary translation. She has written eight books for children and developed many Bibles for children, teens, and adults. She is very active in Calvin Christian Reformed Church and has served on the church council. She has also served on the board of trustees of Calvin Theological Seminary, which led her to attend seminary. She graduated in 2013 with a master's degree in Bible and theology. She loves to work in her Grand Rapids, Michigan, garden and spend time with her young granddaughter.